HOW TO LEAVE PRISON EARLY

Florida Clemency, Parole and Work Release

Reggie Garcia
Lawyer and Lobbyist

Published by:

Laurenzana Press
PO Box 1220
Melrose, FL 32666 USA

www.LaurenzanaPress.com

****

ISBN-13: 978-1-93791883-5

Disclaimer

Nothing contained herein is to be considered as the rendering of legal advice, or the creation of an attorney-client relationship. Readers are responsible for obtaining such advice from their own legal counsel.

This book is intended for educational and informational purposes only. Any testimonials or past results included in this book are based on the specific circumstances of individual cases, and are not intended as a guarantee of future results.

What Others Say...

"The clemency process is one of the most emotional, significant to society and those who are directly affected, and misunderstood undertakings of Florida state government. Mr. Reggie Garcia has spent much of his legal career advising clients and state policy makers on clemency and closely observing its evolution over recent decades. For anyone who wants to understand how the king – now governor and cabinet – dispenses discretionary justice in Florida, this is the book to read."
The Honorable Bob Graham, U.S. Senator 1987-2005;
Governor of Florida 1979-1987 (January 15, 2015)

Reggie Garcia is "an expert in clemency and parole cases."
Sean Rossman, *Tallahassee Democrat* (July 21, 2014)

"A man who <u>truly</u> seeks justice."
Brian Tannebaum, Miami lawyer, author of *The Practice* and past
president of the Florida Association of Criminal Defense Lawyers
(November 18, 2014)

"There is not a more qualified clemency/parole attorney in the State. And yet you took your time to educate me and introduce me to key players. Both [the inmate] and I are so grateful."
Patti Velasquez, Delray Beach lawyer and mediator
(December 1, 2014)

"It's the job of Reggie Garcia (JD '85) to win for his clients the rights and freedoms that no judge or jury can grant."
Richard Goldstein, Editor/ UF Law, in "Official Mercy,"
***UF Law* magazine (Fall 2011)**

"We are so deeply touched by the pure passion, tireless dedication and absolute commitment that Reggie Garcia reflects every day to reverse a decades-old injustice."
Ron Sachs, CEO/Sachs Media Group (August 24, 2014)

"If you want a passionate, capable, knowledgeable attorney on your case, you will find it in Reggie Garcia. He is qualified bar none to take your case before the Florida parole or clemency boards."
Pat Bliss, retired paralegal (September 16, 2014)

DEDICATION

For my beloved parents Elsie and Skip Garcia.
Your careers in health care, law enforcement and politics
inspired my passion for mercy and justice.

TABLE OF CONTENTS

INTRODUCTION

The purpose of *How to Leave Prison Early* is to provide information and inspire action. The target audiences are state prison inmates, their families and supporters, lawyers, and other advocates. It includes the so-called secret sauce (the actual "how-to" steps to leave prison early).

Florida has nearly 101,000 inmates in 49 major state prisons and numerous correctional facilities called annexes and work camps.

A clemency commutation of sentence and parole are alternate paths to the same goal, which is to release the inmate early. Both involve compassion, redemption, and forgiveness, and are the ultimate grant of a second chance. To get either, you must convince elected or appointed officials that the inmate will never commit another serious crime. However, clemency and parole involve different decision-makers, rules and timeframes.

Executive clemency is the governor's power under the Florida Constitution to grant mercy. If the governor says yes, two members of the Florida Cabinet must also agree.

The Florida Cabinet has three members who are elected statewide: Attorney General, Chief Financial Officer, and the Commissioner of Agriculture.

The governor and cabinet serve as the Board of Executive Clemency. If the governor says no, the application is denied which can happen at any time for any reason.

Parole is an act of grace by the state. The power to grant parole is held by the Florida Commission on Offender Review (FCOR or the Commission), formerly known since 1941 as the Florida Parole Commission (FPC). This granting power is derived from general law established by the Florida Legislature that can change the eligibility criteria at any time. The Commission has three appointed members who serve six-year terms.

This book describes the legal and political roadmaps to help inmates, their families and supporters, lawyers, and other advocates learn the options available for early release. It's meant to help them develop a clear goal, realistic plan, and effective strategy to assist a relative or friend get out of prison early.

Community Work Release and **Conditional Medical Release** are also discussed.

Also included is the inspiring and compelling story of an innocent deaf inmate named Felix Garcia (no relation to the author), which is both a clemency and parole case.

Additionally, there are three bonus chapters and a list of definitions to help you understand the sometimes complex roads that must be navigated in advocating for an inmate's early release.

And finally, there's a Call to Action chapter that tells you the first steps on "how-to" get started now.

Discussion of the courts releasing innocent prisoners for newly discovered evidence, like DNA test results, is beyond the scope of this book. However, I encourage you to visit www.floridainnocence.org to learn how the lawyers and investigators of the Innocence Project of Florida fought to get 14 innocent prisoners exonerated and released.

NOTE: Most state prisons in Florida are called "correctional institutions," so they're abbreviated by the prison's name followed by "C.I." The seven privately-managed state prisons are called "correctional facilities," and are abbreviated by the prison's name followed by "C.F."

Why I'm Qualified to Write This Book

As a lawyer and state government lobbyist I...

- Have more than 20 years' experience presenting clemency cases to four Florida governors and numerous cabinet members of both political parties.

- Visited inmates and staff at 29 state prisons.

- Was approved by the Office of Executive Clemency to handle death penalty clemency cases based on a 2014 law.

- Testified before Governor Rick Scott and the Florida Cabinet when the new clemency rules were approved in 2011.

- Met with the commissioners of FCOR and their professional staffs on clemency and parole cases.

- Published legal articles in magazines and opinion editorials (op-eds) in newspapers related to clemency and parole.

- Have given speeches to state associations and community groups on early release strategies.

- Have worked with lawyers and other clemency aides and parole examiners who do the nuts-and-bolts research, and make recommendations on whether to release an inmate early.

- Have appeared on national network and cable television, state and local broadcast affiliate television stations.

- Have been a legal commentator on the radio and published in magazines and newspapers.

- Worked with the Florida Department of Corrections' (FDOC) staff to obtain documents for clemency, parole and administrative prison matters.

- Spoke to correctional officers and inmates in 2004 at the third largest federal women's prison in the country.

- Was appointed as an arbitrator and a court appointed attorney *ad litem* in numerous legal proceedings.

CHAPTER ONE

CLEMENCY AND PAROLE EXPERIENCE

Since 1994, as a lawyer and state government lobbyist I have assisted state prisoners, convicted felons, or other arrested clients with the following legal issues:

- Inmate Felix Garcia who is serving a life sentence to get a three-year parole subsequent interview and a referral for special programs at Wakulla C.I. (See: Chapter Ten)

- Represented a small business owner from Alabama to obtain a full pardon for two 1988 drug convictions.

- After six years of working on a murder case, I argued it before the governor and Florida Cabinet.

- Advocated for an inmate serving a life sentence to get a subsequent parole interview in two years.

- Advocated for an inmate serving a life sentence for two murders to get a parole referral to Wakulla C.I. for special programs.

- Advocated for two inmates serving life sentences to get parole referrals to Sumter C.I. for special programs and a two-year subsequent parole interview.

- Assisted an inmate serving a life sentence for murder to obtain a clemency Request for Review.

- Assisted a Michigan contractor in obtaining a pardon for misdemeanor.

- Advocated for a Tampa Bay certified public accountant to obtain an expedited full pardon.

- Assisted an international business owner and registered sex offender to obtain a waiver and full pardon, negating his duty to register.

- Advocated for an inmate serving life in prison by presenting for him at a waiver hearing.

- Advocated for a Tampa Bay general contractor to obtain Restoration of Civil Rights (RCR) without a hearing.

- Assisted a central Florida international business owner in obtaining a full pardon, including restoration of his firearm authority.

- Assisted a prison inmate convicted of DUI manslaughter in obtaining eligibility approval to seek a waiver and clemency.

- Assisted a prison inmate convicted of first degree murder and serving a life sentence to prepare for a national media network television interview.

- Advocated for an Illinois insurance agent to obtain specific authority to own, possess and use firearms.

- Assisted a major South Florida business owner to obtain an automatic RCR.

- Advocated for a Tampa Bay lawyer to obtain an automatic RCR, enabling him to seek relicensure before the Florida Bar and the Supreme Court of Florida.

- Assisted an inmate to have his 14-year prison sentence for DUI manslaughter commuted to 8 years of time served – one of only 22 commutations approved by Governor Jeb Bush. (See: Chapter Three)

- Assisted a Polk County businessman to obtain RCR.

- Assisted a Clearwater resident to obtain a full pardon.

- Assisted a Broward County public adjuster to obtain RCR.

- Assisted a Brandon business owner to obtain (on the consent agenda) a full pardon.

- Assisted a Riverview electrician to obtain RCR.

- Assisted an inmate to obtain approval for a waiver to seek a commutation of sentence.

- Assisted a Fort Myers general contractor and restaurant owner to obtain RCR.

- Assisted a St. Pete general contractor to obtain RCR.

- Assisted an Ohio business owner of a nursing home and pharmacy convicted of federal health care fraud to obtain RCR without a hearing.

- Assisted a Tallahassee lawyer to obtain RCR.

- Assisted a Miami lawyer to obtain RCR.

- Assisted a Tampa business owner to obtain RCR.

- Assisted an Illinois professional to obtain a pardon without firearm authority.

My First Clemency Case

It seems like yesterday when Tampa lawyer Marcelino J. "Bubba" Huerta called in 1994 and asked me to help a Tampa small business owner obtain firearm authority. All convicted felons lose this right. The client had some minor felony drug and other convictions, but had also been a crime victim.

The Florida Parole Commission's (now called the Florida Commission on Offender Review) advisory recommendation was negative.

There was damaging, inaccurate and incomplete information in the court records, so we had to clarify all the facts and legal issues.

The client owned a small retail business in a high crime area of north Tampa, and handled a significant amount of cash daily. His residence was above the business, so the firearm was to protect his employees, customers and family members.

After conducting our investigation we met with all of the clemency aides to the governor and six cabinet members. (In 2003, after passage of a constitutional amendment, the Florida Cabinet was reduced to the current three members.) Governor Lawton Chiles and the Florida Cabinet approved the firearm authority application.

This case started my interest in and focus on helping convicted felons through the clemency process and later the parole process.

CHAPTER TWO

CLEMENCY – COMMUTATION OF SENTENCE

*"Commutation" basically means to shorten the
sentence given to an inmate.*

Florida Governor Rick Scott and the three statewide elected members of the Florida Cabinet acting as the Board of Executive Clemency (the Board) unanimously approved new clemency rules effective March 9, 2011.[1] The following major changes applied to all pending and new applications for a commutation of a state prison sentence:

- A new Request for Review is a condition precedent, and replaces the previous waiver requirement. The governor plus one cabinet member must approve this request for the applicant to get an investigation and hearing opportunity.

- The inmate must serve one-third of their sentence for any felony conviction, or one-half of the sentence if it is a mandatory minimum sentence, before being eligible to seek a Request for Review.

These major changes replace the April 2007 rules, and are "intended to emphasize public safety and ensure that applicants desire clemency and demonstrate they are unlikely to re-offend."[2]

Inmates still serving state prison terms may seek to have the remainder of their sentence commuted to time served, converted to probation or reduced to a lesser term. Or if a mandatory minimum sentence applies, have it removed to make an inmate eligible for parole.

148 Commutations Have Been Approved[3]

Prison commutations are the most difficult type of clemency to get approved. Since 1980, seven governors and the Board of Executive Clemency have approved 148 commutation applications: (See: Appendix A for a complete list of these cases)

- 21 by Governor Bob Graham (1979–1987)

- 16 by Governor Bob Martinez (1987–1991)

- 65 by the late Governor Lawton Chiles (1991–1998)

- 10 by Governor Buddy MacKay (1998 and 1999)

- 22 by Governor Jeb Bush (1999–2007)

- 13 by Governor Charlie Crist (2007–2011)

- 1 by Governor Rick Scott (2011–present)

These clemency rules explain in more detail what a commutation means and who is eligible:

Clemency Rule 4.D. states:
"A commutation of sentence may adjust an applicant's penalty *to one less severe* but does not restore any civil right, and it does not restore the authority to own, possess, or use firearms."

Clemency Rule 5.B. regarding eligibility to apply for a commutation states:
"A person *may not* be considered for a commutation of sentence unless...he has been *granted a Request for Review* pursuant to Rule 8 or has had his case placed upon a Clemency Board agenda pursuant to Rule 17."

Clemency Rule 8.A. provides an inmate applicant who receives a *mandatory minimum sentence* **must serve at least** *one-half* **of their sentence and all other applicants must serve one-third of their**

The clemency meetings to consider prison commutations are public meetings at the state capitol in Tallahassee, Florida. They are attended by victims and their family members, state attorneys, law enforcement, advocacy groups and the media. (Think of it as a big school board or county commission meeting.)

The applicant is in state prison and is not allowed to personally appear before the Board. The applicant's family, lawyer and other supporters represent the inmate who may submit written information for consideration.

Expediting a Case for "Exceptional Merit" Per Rule 17

Clemency Rule 17 provides that in cases of "exceptional merit" any member of the Board may place a clemency case on an upcoming agenda for consideration. Only time will tell how often Board members exercise this prerogative. Also unclear is whether Rule 17 will be used only to expedite pending applications, or if time-ineligible persons can be considered.

25 Proactive Steps That Can Make a Difference

Every case is different, but these 25 proactive "how-to" steps help increase chances of success in a clemency application:

Phase 1:

☐ 1. Review the inmate's felony conviction documents, including the police report, probable cause affidavit, charging instrument (direct filed information or grand jury indictment), judgment, and sentence, autopsy report, court transcripts, appellate record and legal briefs.

☐ 2. Review the inmate's Florida Department of Law Enforcement (FDLE) criminal history.

☐ 3. Review any public records related to the inmate from the Florida Department of Corrections (FDOC).

☐ 4. Review the inmate's complete driving record from Florida Department of Highway Safety and Motor Vehicles (FDHSMV).

☐ 5. Determine and confirm with the clemency staff the inmate's clemency eligibility.

☐ 6. Interview the inmate and family.

☐ 7. Interview the plea, trial and appellate lawyers.

☐ 8. Determine the legal and political viability of the case.

Phase 2:

☐ 9. Obtain from the applicable Clerk of Court certified copies of court records.

☐ 10. Prepare and hand–deliver the clemency application and certified records.

☐ 11. Prepare an advocacy letter describing mitigating factors, rehabilitation since the conviction, and the six approval "factors."

☐ 12. Assist to obtain character and support letters.

☐ 13. Determine if the case has "exceptional merit."

☐ 14. Meet with the governor's clemency lawyers and other clemency aides to answer questions and advocate for approval.

Phase 3:

☐ 15. Prepare for the inmate's interview with the parole examiner.

☐ 16. Provide information to, and meet with, the three members of the Florida Commission on Offender Review to encourage a positive advisory recommendation.

☐ 17. Coordinate with inmate's supporters.

☐ 18. Provide continuing legal counsel and advice.

☐ 19. Provide written clarification of any issues raised during the investigation.

☐ 20. Review the Confidential Case Analysis and advisory recommendation.

☐ 21. Contact the governor's legal counsel and other clemency aides prior to the clemency board meeting.

☐ 22. Submit the notification to reserve time to speak at the upcoming meeting.

☐ 23. Select witnesses, and otherwise prepare for and attend the clemency hearing.

☐ 24. Coordinate any follow-up communications required during the process or after the clemency meeting, including obtaining the letter or executive order describing the decision.

☐ 25. Regardless of the decision, write to thank the governor, cabinet members and their clemency aides.

This list may feel overwhelming, so just take one step at a time. Be patient as seeking justice, grace and mercy is not a fast or easy process.

CHAPTER THREE

CASE STUDY – INMATE LEAVES PRISON SIX YEARS EARLY

As discussed in Chapter Two, a commutation of sentence is the hardest type of executive clemency to obtain – and it should be. While maintaining the confidentiality of all parties, this chapter discusses an example of a successfully completed case to show how we were able to get a state prison inmate released six years early.

It was the summer of 1998 in the Florida Panhandle. Unfortunately, like too many cases a 17-year old female passenger died in a car accident due to a drunk driver. The driver was 19 and a "good kid from a good family." They were friends and were on spring break with a group of high school and college kids who'd been drinking and partying for several days.

A passenger in my client's car, the deceased young lady was also a "good kid from a good family." As they were driving at three o'clock in the morning to get food, he rear-ended another car which caused the fatal accident.

My client's blood alcohol level (BAL) was 0.112 (in Florida you're presumed intoxicated with a BAL of 0.08 or more). He tried to help his injured friend, but sadly she died at the scene.

He cooperated with officials and pled to the crime, and received a 14-year sentence in the state prison to be followed by one year of probation. The deceased girl's mother had asked for the maximum prison sentence of 15 years. Her only child had just been killed, so her position was what any grieving parent would request.

Once my client served five years, we filed a clemency case and worked on it for three years. He had a model prison record, strong family and community support, and agreed that if he was released early to NEVER drink and drive again.

By following many of the 25 "how-to" steps listed in Chapter Two, we reached a successful outcome. In 2006, Governor Jeb Bush and the Florida Cabinet approved releasing my client six years early, and converted his remaining prison time to probation.

Once the mother of the deceased young lady learned he had been a model inmate, she did not oppose the commutation for which we were very grateful. This case was a good and fair result.

My client is currently gainfully employed, raising a family, and has never re-offended. Plus, he speaks to high school and college students about the dangers of drinking and driving.

DUI manslaughter cases, or any death case, are especially difficult because the victim's surviving family has to re-live the accident, the crime, and their relative's death during clemency (or parole) proceedings.

(See: Appendix A for examples of other cases that resulted in prison commutations.)

CHAPTER FOUR

PAROLE – AN ACT OF GRACE

Parole is a discretionary release and an act of grace from the state.[4] No inmate can claim a right to parole.[5] Parole's phase-out began in 1983 when the Supreme Court of Florida approved sentencing guidelines that became applicable to most felonies committed after October 1, 1983.[6] Parole remained in effect for capital murder and sexual battery until October 1, 1995.[7]

Since 2011, I have argued five murder cases and one sexual battery case at parole hearings in Tallahassee, Florida.

As of June 2014, there are 4,626 inmates who are eligible for parole. Most of these inmates have received life sentences, and are required to serve a minimum of 25 years before becoming eligible for parole.

So, who is a good candidate for parole? First and foremost, the inmate must no longer be a safety threat to the community. Additionally:

- Some inmates are innocent and were wrongfully convicted.

- Other inmates had minor roles, and were given long sentences disproportionate to those given to more culpable codefendants.

- Many were young at the time of their crimes and have been model inmates.

- In some cases, the victim's family shows compassion and supports the inmate's release.

This chapter describes the long, technical, and complicated process of attempting to obtain an inmate's release on parole. It also encourages inmates, their families, and their lawyers to have a strategy, a plan, and realistic expectations.

Three Commissioners

The Florida Commission on Offender Review (the Commission) is a state agency comprised of three commissioners who make post-release decisions affecting inmates and ex-offenders. The Commission, an administrative agency, functions as a quasi-judicial body. It also investigates clemency applications and makes advisory recommendations.

Appointed by the governor and Florida Cabinet, and confirmed by the Florida Senate, the commissioners are appointed for six-year terms.[8] The current chair of the Commission is Tena M. Pate who was appointed by Governor Bush in 2003, and reappointed by Governor Crist and Governor Scott in 2011. One of the most respected officials in state government, Chair Pate previously served as Florida's Victims' Rights Coordinator for Governors Bush, Chiles, and MacKay, as well as for the state attorney in the First Judicial Circuit.

Vice-Chair and Commissioner Melinda N. Coonrod was appointed by Governor Scott in July, 2012 for a six-year term. She is a distinguished lawyer, a former state prosecutor for six years in the Second Judicial Circuit, and the former supervising hearing officer at the Florida Department of Agriculture and Consumer Services presiding over hundreds of administrative license cases.

Secretary and Commissioner Richard D. Davison is the newest member. He was appointed by Governor Scott in August, 2014 for a six-year term. Commissioner Davison will be considered for confirmation by the Florida Senate in the spring 2015. A lawyer and former prosecutor, Commissioner Davison is a well-respected former deputy secretary of the Department of Corrections and the Department of Juvenile Justice.

Commissioners are limited to two consecutive six-year terms.[9] Somewhat unique to state government, retired and former commissioners may preside over cases when a current commissioner is unavailable or there is a temporary opening.[10] Hearings are held most Wednesdays in Tallahassee, and occasionally in various Florida counties.[11]

Types of Hearings

1. **Initial Interview:** Parole will not be considered. The purpose of this hearing is only to establish a Presumptive Parole Release Date (PPRD) and the Next Interview Date (NID). The Commission evaluates many factors in establishing the PPRD.[12]

2. **Request for Review:** This review considers every matter with which the inmate takes issue or exception (i.e., the salient factor score, severity of offense behavior, aggravating or mitigating factors, etc.) regarding the establishment of their PRRD. To obtain this review, the inmate must first file a request within 60 days of the Commission Action after the initial hearing.[13]

3. **Subsequent Interview:** This interview determines if any changes should be made in the PPRD and establishes the NID. The Commission can elect to make no change, to reduce, or extend the PPRD.[14]

4. **Effective Interview:** This interview determines whether the inmate will be granted parole. The Commission can elect to grant parole, extend the PPRD, or decline to authorize parole.[15]

5. **Extraordinary Review:** This hearing is to review an order outlining the reasons for the Commission's decision to decline to authorize parole. The Commission can elect to move the order to suspend the PPRD and schedule the NID, grant parole, or extend the PPRD.[16]

6. **Extraordinary Interview:** When the PPRD is in suspended status, the inmate receives an Extraordinary Interview to determine if the inmate's PPRD should be removed from a

suspended status. The Commission can elect to make no change in the PPRD, establish an Effective Parole Release Date (EPRD) within the next two years, or grant parole.[17]

7. **Parole Supervision Review:** This hearing reviews the parolee's progress while on parole. The Commission may elect to make no change or modify the reporting schedule and/or conditions of parole and schedule the next review date.[18]

Recent Approvals

As of June 30, 2014 there were 4,626 inmates eligible for parole. During the three fiscal years from 2011 to 2014, the Commission granted parole to 95 inmates after considering 978 who were eligible.[19]

For those unapproved inmates, the key questions are: 1) When will they be interviewed again?; and 2) Do they have a realistic opportunity to ever be paroled?

In addition to the inmate's crime and prison record, the two most important considerations are the opinions of the victim and the victim's family, and the state attorney's position.

Presumptive Parole Release Date (PPRD)

The PPRD is defined by Florida law, and is the tentative parole release date as determined by objective parole guidelines.[20] The "objective parole guidelines" reflect the name of the 1978 parole law per Section 947.165 of the Florida Statutes, and constitute the criteria upon which parole decisions are made.[21]

The Florida Legislature delegated this authority to the Commission, requiring only that it be based on an acceptable research model on the seriousness of the offense and on the likelihood of a favorable parole outcome.[22]

Guidelines

The Commission's current objective parole guidelines became effective in September 1981. The following guidelines or considerations are still being used, but can be revised by the Legislature at any time.[23]

After the parole examiner interviews the inmate, writes a report and makes a recommendation, the commissioners determine the following:

- salient factor score

- offense severity level

- matrix time range

- aggravating and mitigating factors

- "institutional conduct record" and program participation.

Using these guidelines, the commissioners calculate the number of months from the start of the sentence to establish the PPRD. The Commission can affirm or modify this date at subsequent hearings.[24] These guidelines involve statutory, administrative, and policy considerations.

Affirmative "Finding" Needed for Release

While good institutional conduct, a lack of disciplinary reports, and successful completion of programs are positive indicators, the law actually says "no person shall be placed on parole merely as a reward for good conduct or efficient performance of duties assigned in prison." [25]

Instead, the commissioners must make an affirmative finding that "there is reasonable probability that, if the person is placed on parole, he or she will live and conduct him or herself as a respectable and law-abiding person and that the person's release will be compatible with his or her own welfare and the welfare of society." [26]

The "Subsequent" Hearing

At the initial and every subsequent hearing, the most important decision made is when to re-review the case. The next review can be scheduled within as few as two years, or as many as seven years from the last review. This is the best indicator of whether the Commission is willing to consider a future parole release.

Effective July 1, 2013, the law increased the intervals between parole interview dates from two to seven years for inmates convicted of kidnapping or attempted kidnapping, robbery, certain burglaries, or breaking and entering, or an attempt thereof of any of these crimes "in which a human being is present and a sexual act is attempted or completed." [27]

It's estimated that these changes will impact less than 50 inmates, and the Commission will maintain its considerable discretion as to scheduling subsequent interviews. While not stated in the new law or its Final Bill Analysis, the legislative intent likely was to reduce the number of hearings crime victims and/or their families have to attend.

Special "Re-Entry" Programs

Another important decision is whether the Commission recommends program participation for inmates at Everglades C.I. in Miami (aka: the FIU Corrections Transition Program); Sumter C.I. in Bushnell; or Wakulla C.I. in Crawfordville near Tallahassee.

Wakulla is the state's first "Faith-and Character-Based Prison." Successful completion of these specialized and intensive re-entry programs is essentially a condition precedent to any eventual parole release.

17 Suggested Proactive Steps

Every case is different, but these 17 proactive "how-to" steps help increase chances of success in requesting parole for an inmate:

☐ 1. The inmate must stay out of trouble. Period! This means no disciplinary reports and no excuses!

☐ 2. Obtain and review inmate records from the FDOC.

☐ 3. Prepare the inmate's prison resume to include certificates or letters for programs completed: work experience and skills; GED education; vocational training; faith-based program participation; alcohol and substance abuse training; financial literacy; college; mentoring; and any other special accomplishments or achievements.

☐ 4. Several months in advance, call and write (via email or letter or both) the commissioners' staffs to confirm the upcoming prison interview.

☐ 5. Prepare the inmate for the prison interview by the parole examiner. This is the inmate's only opportunity to personally make their case.

☐ 6. Ask for and read the staff parole report. Though it is the formal recommendation, the commissioners are not bound by it.

☐ 7. Write all commissioners to clarify or dispute any inaccurate information in their staff report.

☐ 8. At least 60 days prior to the parole hearing, prepare and mail an advocacy letter on WHY the inmate deserves parole. Describe the release plan including housing; jobs; health care; transportation; alcohol or substance abuse counseling; family, community and faith activities and support, etc.

☐ 9. Ask the Commission's Victim Advocate to share the advocacy letter and any apology letter with the victim's family.

☐ 10. Send a copy of the advocacy letter and the inmate's prison resume to the current elected state attorney where the crime was prosecuted. Florida's 20 elected state attorneys are always contacted by the Commission's staff. They usually take a formal position against the inmate's parole, either by appearing at the hearing or writing a letter or both.

☐ 11. Confirm the hearing date, time and location, and arrive in Tallahassee the night before to be rested and prepared.

☐ 12. With only ten (10) minutes to address the commissioners, select the best family member or character supporter to present the case. No more than two people should speak, but bringing additional supporters is a good idea. Remember, for security reasons the inmate is not allowed to attend the hearing.

☐ 13. Arrive early, sign in at the hearing with the clerk, and check the docket list to determine the number and anticipated time of the inmate's case.

☐ 14. When the case is called, speak clearly, and make a compelling argument why the inmate deserves parole by using the key points from the advocacy letter. You should ASK the commissioners for:

- a specific next interview date of two or three years;

- special programming at a certain prison (usually Everglades, Sumter or Wakulla); and

- a favorable presumptive parole release date.

☐ 15. Regardless of the decision, thank the commissioners and staff, exit the hearing room, and ask the staff clerk any questions you might have if you did not hear or understand the decision.

☐ 16. After you receive the Commissioner's Action Report describing the decision, write the clerk to request clarification of any part of the decision that you don't understand.

☐ 17. Before all subsequent interviews, hearings, and any reviews, repeat and refine steps 1 through 16 above, focusing your advocacy on the inmate's progress since the last hearing or review.

(See: Chapter 8 to learn more about the three commissioners, and how to contact them and the Commission's staff. And Appendix C for a list of approved transitional housing.)

Different than "Executive Clemency"

Parole is different than "executive clemency." Clemency is a power vested in the governor and Florida Cabinet by the Florida Constitution.[28]

As discussed in Chapter 2, clemency may include a commutation of sentence which requires approval by the governor and two members of the Florida Cabinet.[29] Since 1980, there have been 148 commutations of sentences granted by seven governors and numerous members of the Florida Cabinet.[30]

CHAPTER FIVE

COMMUNITY WORK RELEASE

Good for Florida's Inmates and Taxpayers

Separate from clemency or parole, community work release presents the best opportunity to leave prison early.

There are nearly 101,000 inmates in Florida's 49 major state prisons and numerous annexes, work camps, work release centers, and other correctional facilities. These include five intake reception and medical centers in Miami, Orlando, Ocala, Lake Butler, and Chipley, as well as seven privately-operated facilities.

The Florida Department of Corrections (FDOC) is Florida's largest state agency, and the third largest state prison system in the country with a $2.1 billion budget and 22,400 employees. The FDOC secretary is appointed by the governor and confirmed by the Florida Senate.[31] In December 2014, Julie Jones was appointed secretary. Secretary Jones is one of the most respected and accomplished senior executives in state government. This position is arguably the hardest job in state government.

During the next 12 months one-third of these 101,000 inmates will be released on their end of sentence date. Some inmates are eligible for work release during the last 14 to 36 months before their sentences end.

Since space must be available – and there are numerous safety, transportation and security considerations – in reality work release is usually only available the last six to nine months of an inmate's sentence.

Waiting lists are common. Currently there are around 4,000 inmates participating in 35 work release programs at 21 private and 14 public locations throughout Florida.[32]

(See: Appendix B that lists the 35 locations of work release centers in three regions of the state.)

What is 'Work Release'?

Formally known as "community work release," this term refers to the portion of the community release program that allows inmates to work at paid employment in the community while continuing as inmates of the facility where they are required to be confined.[33] It is commonly referred to as "work release," and it is the key transition and re-entry component of the broader community release program (CRP).

The CRP refers to "...any program that allows inmates to work at paid employment, a center work assignment, or to participate in education, training, substance abuse treatment programs, or any other transitional program to facilitate re-entry into the community while in a work release center, contract community work release facility, or other state-contracted community facility." [34]

The Five Policy Goals of Work Release [35]

1. Gradual reintegration back into the community.

2. Gainful employment.

3. Accumulation of savings from paid employment.

4. Preservation of family and community ties.

5. Participation in self-help programs.

Who is Eligible and Why?

An inmate must meet established criteria in order to be considered for placement in a work release center. The inmate must be in FDOC's custody for at least 60 days; have no disqualifying convictions or events; have no disciplinary history for 60 days prior to placement; and otherwise be classified as being under "community custody." [36]

Additionally, an inmate must be within these specific timeframes:[37]

Inmates with non-advanceable dates must be:

- Within 28 months of the earliest tentative release date for the community-based residential transition program (pre-work release);

- Within 19 months of the tentative release date or "presumptive parole release date" for center work assignment and community-based residential substance abuse program; or

- Within 14 months of the earliest tentative release date for work release.

Inmates without non-advanceable dates must be:

- Within 36 months of the earliest tentative release date for the community-based residential transition program (pre-work release);

- Within 28 months of the tentative release date for center work assignment and community-based residential substance abuse program; or

- Within 19 months of the tentative release date for work release.

The term "non-advanceable dates" refers to an inmate's release date that is restricted from continuous monthly gain time awards over the entire length of sentence. This complicated calculation involves certain crimes after October 1, 1995; any "presumptive parole release date"; and certain mandatory minimum sentences by re-offenders.[38]

Public Safety's Seven Factors [39]

Besides the formal eligibility criteria, with inherent discretion by FDOC's senior management and staff, the following approval factors are considered to ensure the public safety of citizens, employers, correctional officers and other inmates:

1. What is the inmate's arrest history? Are there any violent offenses, including actual or attempted sex crimes?

2. Are there pending outside charges such as active arrest warrants or detainers by state or federal law enforcement agencies?

3. Are there prison disciplinary history and reports, especially any involving violence, attempted escapes, substance abuse or sexual acts?

4. What is the inmate's alcohol, drug and other substance abuse history?

5. What are the inmate's program needs, including re-entry considerations?

6. Where will the inmate be located? And are there other concerns of the crime's victim(s)?

7. What are the inmate's skills, physical ability and overall compatibility with the specifically-requested CRP?

Common Sense Proactive Steps

As indicated by the policy goals, eligibility requirements, and safety factors, "how-to" get approved for work release is driven by many considerations. The inmate's focus, determination, persistence, common sense, and some good luck and timing all play a part in approval for work release.

To increase the chances of being selected, <u>the inmate should</u>:

☐ 1. Again, stay out of trouble. Period. No excuses!

☐ 2. Learn the work release rules, and tell the classification officer the inmate has a strong desire for participation.

☐ 3. Prepare a prison resume to include all certificates and letters of accomplishments, and update it as new programs are completed.

☐ 4. Tell the classification officers, work supervisors and program teachers of the inmate's interest in work release. The inmate must then listen and get advice on how to be selected.

☐ 5. Be patient. While the law and rules indicate many inmates are *eligible* during the last 14 to 36 months, the reality is every eligible inmate cannot be accommodated. These coveted slots have to be EARNED.

☐ 6. Request that family members, supporters and prospective employers write the inmate's classification officer to encourage approval for work release.

☐ 7. Finally, if and when selected, the inmate should be grateful for the opportunity, follow the work release rules, and do a good job. This formula will keep the inmate in the program and validate FDOC's selection of the inmate.

Many Inmates Are Not Eligible ... Nor Should They Be

Florida laws, administrative rules and FDOC's policies prevent violent inmates, sex offenders, and certain other high-risk inmates from ever being eligible.

There are nine disqualifying crimes, and other criteria dictated by formal administrative rules.[40] Obvious issues like an attempted escape or a termination from prior work release programs should be disqualifiers; while other factors like a minor disciplinary report or overdue child support payments should be considered on a case-by-case basis, and should not be automatic disqualifiers.[41]

Cost Savings and Restitution [42]

Ninety-five percent of FDOC's $2.1 billion budget is comprised of three major service delivery functions:

- 66% for security and institutional operations, which includes 15,000 correctional officers and supervisors, and 2,400 support staff.

- 19% for health services, which includes 1,500 medical and support personnel.

- 10% for community corrections, which includes 2,000 correctional probation officers who police 145,000 offenders on community supervision commonly known as just probation. Offenders may be on probation instead of or after state prison.

Besides the obvious fact that Florida's taxpayers and visitors fund corrections, corrections-related activities, and all other state government functions through sales, property and other taxes, we all have a vested interest in work release programs being successful and expanded. From paying taxes and preventing recidivism, to public safety and an individual's positive participation in society, work release programs are effective, less expensive than continued incarceration, and must be carefully managed for success.

The average inmate costs of $48 per day (described by FDOC as "per diem") ranges between $28 to $89 depending on where the inmate is located.

Work release programs are the best option for an inmate, and are the most cost-effective for the state. There are eight types of correctional facilities and programs with significant daily cost differentials, as follows:

- Work Release Centers - $28
- Contracted Facility - $29
- Adult Male Custody - $37
- Private Institutions - $44
- Specialty Institutions - $53

- Adult and Youthful Female Custody - $53
- Male Youthful Offender - $64
- Reception and Medical Centers - $89

Throughout the work release process, inmates pay 55% of their earnings for subsistence. They must also use 10% of their net pay for court-ordered restitution, fees and costs. Clearly, work release centers are the least expensive to operate daily, yet only 4% of inmates are in these programs.

P.R.I.D.E. = Rehabilitation*

The acronym PRIDE stands for "Prison Rehabilitative Industries and Diversified Enterprises, Inc." Although different than work release, PRIDE has similar goals, and the two programs are not mutually exclusive.

Created in 1981 by the Florida Legislature as a private, not-for-profit inmate training program, in 2013 PRIDE trained almost 3,600 inmates in 42 diverse industries in 20 correctional institutions.

PRIDE inmates worked almost 3.5 million hours and trained in modern high-technology trades such as print and digital information, garments and apparel, furniture manufacturing, vehicle renovation, metal fabrication, dental, and optical services.

With more than 30 years of experience, PRIDE's post-release track record is impressive: 63% of PRIDE-trained former inmates were placed in "relevant jobs," and only 11% re-offended and returned to prison.[43] This successful national model was the brain child of drugstore owner and visionary Jack Eckerd.

Disclosure: In 1994, the author was a federal lobbyist for PRIDE working on labor and compensation issues.

Faith-and Character-Based (FCB) and Re-Entry Prisons

The Florida Legislature and FDOC are laser-focused on increasing and improving re-entry programs. In addition to, and often working in

coordination with, the 35 work release centers, the FDOC has numerous education, work, training and self-improvement courses at most
facilities. There are approximately 6,500 inmates at 16 Florida Faith-
and-Character-Based (FCB) prisons. The largest, with 3,500 inmates, is
Wakulla C.I. and Annex located south of Tallahassee. First implemented
by former Governor Jeb Bush in 1999, it is a successful model for Florida
and other states.

The other major FCB prisons are Tomoka C.I. in Daytona; Hernan-
do C.I. for women in Brooksville; and Lawtey C.I. in North Florida.[44]

With the goal of successful transitions back into communities and
to reduce recidivism, the FDOC and private contractors operate five
designated re-entry facilities at Baker C.I. (North Florida, west of Jacksonville); Polk C.I. (Central Florida); Sago Palm Re-Entry Facility (in
western Palm Beach County); Gadsden Re-Entry Facility (in North
Florida, west of Tallahassee; and a new one at Everglades C.I. (in South
Florida).

These prisons partner with local law enforcement agencies and non-
profits, utilize state and federal grants, and work with re-entry portals to
help soon-to-be-released inmates be ready to work and succeed.[45]

Recent Legislation

In 2014, the Florida Legislature passed a new law to help inmates
obtain a certified birth certificate copy and a state identification card,
often a first step to obtain housing, jobs and to continue in community
substance abuse programs.[46]

In 2013 the Florida Legislature: 1) limited private work release
centers to a maximum of 200 inmates, and required at least one correctional officer in facilities with more than 100 inmates, and 2) funded
$3.8 million for FDOC to "provide electronic monitoring for inmates in
privately operated work release facilities while in the community under
work release assignment." [47]

The 2013 law changes were a result of an inmate escaping from the
Largo Residential Re-Entry Center and murdering two Pinellas County
residents, and a second inmate committing a sexual assault and an attempted murder.

CHAPTER SIX

CONDITIONAL MEDICAL RELEASE FOR INMATES WITH A PERMANENT INCAPACITY OR TERMINAL ILLNESS

While clemency, parole and work release get more media attention and generate the most legal questions, there is another way to leave prison early. The Florida Commission on Offender Review has the exclusive power to release a very ill inmate early. Florida Law 947.149, in part, states:

947.149 Conditional medical release

1) The commission shall, in conjunction with the department, establish the conditional medical release program. An inmate is eligible for consideration for release under the conditional medical release program when the inmate, because of an existing medical or physical condition, is determined by the department to be within one of the following designations:

    (a) "<u>Permanently incapacitated inmate</u>," which means an inmate who has a condition caused by injury, disease, or illness which, to a reasonable degree of medical certainty, renders the inmate permanently and irreversibly physically incapacitated to the extent that the inmate does not constitute a danger to herself or himself or others.

(b) "Terminally ill inmate," which means an inmate who has a
condition caused by injury, disease, or illness which, to a
reasonable degree of medical certainty, renders the inmate
terminally ill to the extent that there can be no recovery and
death is imminent, so that the inmate does not constitute a
danger to herself or himself or others.

No inmate has a right to conditional medical release or to a medical
evaluation to determine eligibility for such release. Inmates sentenced to
death are not eligible.

Since 1996, there have been only 204 inmates approved for a "conditional medical release." [48]

Since 2011, two private companies started providing medical care
to inmates. This may further complicate and delay these medical evaluations.

Conditional Medical Releases from
Fiscal Year 1996–1997 to Fiscal Year 2013–2014

Fiscal Year (July 1–June 30)	Total
FY 1996–1997	19
FY 1997–1998	9
FY 1998–1999	6
FY1999–2000	10
FY 2000–2001	16
FY 2001–2002	15
FY 2002–2003	4
FY 2003–2004	9
FY 2004–2005	12
FY 2005–2006	14
FY 2006–2007	8
FY 2007–2008	10
FY 2008–2009	19
FY 2009–2010	8
FY 2010–2011	16
FY 2011–2012	16
FY 2012–2013	7
FY 2013–2014	6
Total	204

The Florida Department of Corrections' (FDOC) doctors and medical staff have the power to diagnose the inmate and make a preliminary determination that an inmate is "permanently incapacitated" or "terminally ill," and thus qualified for a conditional medical release. FDOC then is supposed to make an actual "referral" to the Commission that has the sole discretion to approve or deny any release.

The FDOC's referral must include:

- a **clinical report** with the complete medical information justifying a release, and

- a **verifiable release plan** describing the medical care and attention needed.

Besides Florida Law 947.149, six Florida administrative rules[49] describe the specific implementation details regarding:

- Eligibility

- Victim input

- Standard and special conditions

- Postponement and rescission

- Revocation

As far as "how-to" increase the inmate's chances of being granted a conditional medical release, these four steps should be taken:

1. Family members, lawyers and other advocates who best know the inmate's medical condition should visit frequently.

2. Encourage the FDOC to recommend the inmate's release through calls, emails and letters to the warden and classification officer.

3. Be persistent, especially if the inmate's medical condition declines.

4. Offer to provide a private doctor to diagnose the inmate.

With nearly 101,000 inmates in state prison (including 21% over the age of 50), the reality is there are thousands of older inmates with chronic illnesses. While very serious, most of these illnesses evidently do not rise to the level of having a terminal illness or permanent incapacitation.

Of this group there are 1,100 inmates age 70 or older, many of whom have the most severe age-related medical conditions and are the lowest security risk. Because of their advanced age, the cost of providing medical care to this group is very expensive compared to the general inmate population.

During the calendar years 2011 to 2014, approximately 1,183 male prisoners and 73 female prisoners of all ages have died mostly of natural causes such as:

- Diseases of the digestive system, including chronic liver disease and cirrhosis.

- Diabetes, pneumonia, respiratory arrest, multi-system organ failure, kidney disease and infections.

While other inmates died from one of the following:

- Cancer

- Cardiac disease

- Accidents

- HIV

- Homicide

- Suicide

Without further medical and legal research of individual cases, it's impossible to know whether any of these inmates would have qualified for a conditional medical release.

The FDOC should allow families to hire private doctors to examine and diagnose the inmate. While these private clinical reports and recommendations will not be binding on the FDOC or the Commission, it will provide additional valuable information for consideration at no expense to the state.

During the fall of 2014, the FDOC disclosed that more than 100 recent inmate deaths are being investigated by the Florida Department of Law Enforcement, the state's top police agency. Thus, it is likely some of the "natural causes" deaths may be re-categorized in the future.

Prompted by suspicious inmate deaths and extensive media reporting, these extraordinary outside police reviews suggest some of the FDOC's internal inspector general investigations need outside and more detailed reviews.

CHAPTER SEVEN

CONTACT THE DECISION-MAKERS: WHO AND HOW?

THE GOVERNOR AND FLORIDA CABINET
(AKA: THE BOARD OF EXECUTIVE CLEMENCY)

Office of Executive Clemency

Since most inmates can't afford a lawyer, Chapters 7 and 8 describe who to contact and how to contact them. Inmates can write letters, and family members and other advocates can make other contacts on behalf of the inmates.

Under Florida law all correspondence sent to the governor's office (which is not exempt or confidential pursuant to Chapter 119 of the Florida Statutes) is a public record.

All public record electronic mail (email) sent through this website will be posted to Project Sunburst at http://www.flgov.com/sunburst and will be accessible to the public. (If you don't want the public record contents of your email or your email address to be published on this website, or to be provided to the public in response to a public records request, do not send an email to this entity).

Be aware that personal information sent in correspondence, such as home addresses and telephone numbers, may be posted to the Sunburst public records website.

All written information may be sent directly to:

The Office of Executive Clemency
Julia McCall, Coordinator
4070 Esplanade Way
Tallahassee, FL 32399-2450

Toll Free: 1-800-435-8286
Phone: (850) 488-2952
Fax: (850) 488-0695
Email: Clemencyweb@fpc.state.fl.us
Website: https://www.fcor.state.fl.us/clemency.shtml

Florida Clemency Rule 16

Florida Clemency Rule 16 governs confidentiality of information presented to the board:

Confidentiality of Records and Documents:
Due to the nature of the information presented to the Clemency Board, all records and documents generated and gathered in the clemency process as set forth in the Rules of Executive Clemency are confidential and shall not be made available for inspection to any person except members of the Clemency Board and their staff. Only the governor, and no other member of the Clemency Board, nor any other state entity that may be in the possession of Clemency Board materials, has the discretion to allow such records and documents to be inspected or copied. Access to such materials, as approved by the governor, does not constitute a waiver of confidentiality.

Governor Rick Scott

Executive Office of Governor Rick Scott
400 S. Monroe Street
Tallahassee, FL 32399
(850) 488-7146

Email: Rick.Scott@eog.myflorida.com

Website: http://www.flgov.com/

Biography

Rick Scott is the 45th Governor of the great State of Florida. As promised during his campaign, Scott is focused on creating jobs and turning Florida's economy around.

Born in Bloomington, Illinois, and raised in Kansas City, Missouri, his father was in the 82nd Airborne during World War II. After the war, Gov. Scott's father was a city bus driver and then a truck driver. His mother worked as a J. C. Penney clerk. At times the family struggled financially, and when Gov. Scott started public school, they lived in public housing.

In high school, Gov. Scott met Ann, and the high school sweethearts have been married for 42 years and have two married daughters, Allison and Jordan, and three grandsons, Auguste, Quinton and Sebastian.

After attending high school and community college, Gov. Scott enlisted in the United States Navy, where he served on active duty aboard the USS Glover as a radar man. The G.I. Bill enabled Gov. Scott to attend college and law school.

While enrolled at the University of Missouri-Kansas City and working full-time at a local grocery store, Gov. Scott and Ann made their first significant foray into the business world by buying two Kansas City doughnut shops for Gov. Scott's mother to manage. Following graduation from UMKC with a degree in business administration, Gov. Scott earned a law degree from Southern Methodist University.

After law school, Gov. Scott stayed in Dallas, working for the city's largest law firm, Johnson & Swanson, primarily representing companies in the health care, oil and gas and communication industries.

In 1987, while still practicing law, Gov. Scott made an offer to purchase HCA, Inc. When the offer was rejected, Gov. Scott started Columbia Hospital Corporation with his and Ann's entire life savings of $125,000.

Gov. Scott also started Conservatives for Patient's Rights, which advocated for free market principles of choice, competition, accountability and personal responsibility in health care. Gov. Scott wanted to prevent further government encroachment on the rights of patients.

When Gov. Scott left Columbia in 1997 at age 44, it was one of the most admired companies in America. It had grown to become the world's largest health care company with more than 340 hospitals, 135 surgery centers, and 550 home health locations in 37 states and two foreign countries. Columbia employed more than 285,000 people, making it the 7th largest U.S. employer and the 12th largest employer worldwide.

Faith, Family and Community

Before moving to Tallahassee, the Scott family lived in Naples. When they are back home, they still attend Naples Community Church, which Rick and Ann helped start in 2006.

Throughout their lives, Gov. Scott and First Lady Ann have served their community through volunteer and charitable work. Rick has served on the National Board of the United Way, and Gov. Scott and Ann have worked with World Vision to create a primary health care system in Bunyala, a poor area of Kenya.

In addition, they fund scholarships for graduates of the Kansas City high school they both attended, as well as one that enables a low-income student to attend SMU Law School each year. They also fund an entrepreneur contest at George Washington University where one of their daughters received a business degree.

Businessman and Entrepreneur

Gov. Scott is known as an innovator in business, health care, and politics. His specialization was in health care mergers and acquisitions, and it was during his work on these transactions that he recognized how patients could be better served by improving hospital efficiency, lowering costs, and focusing on better outcomes.

Through his entrepreneurship, Gov. Scott developed a reputation in the health care industry for providing affordable, high quality care to patients. As Governor, he brings a similar vision for quality and efficiency to benefit the people of Florida.

Attorney General Pam Bondi

Office of Attorney General
State of Florida
The Capitol PL-01
Tallahassee, FL 32399-1050
(850) 414-3300

Email: Pam.Bondi@myfloridalegal.com

Website: http://www.myfloridalegal.com/

Biography

A native of Tampa, Pam Bondi became Florida's 37th Attorney General after being elected on November 2, 2010. Attorney General Bondi was sworn in to office January 4, 2011.

Attorney General Bondi is focused on protecting Floridians and upholding Florida's laws and its Constitution. Some of her top priorities are: defending Florida's constitutional rights against the federal health care law; strengthening penalties to stop pill mills; aggressively investigating mortgage fraud and Medicaid fraud; and ensuring Florida is compensated for Deepwater Horizon oil spill losses. Transparency and openness in government have been important throughout her career, and Attorney General Bondi continues to support Florida's Sunshine laws.

Attorney General Bondi is dedicated to serving her community, including her membership on the Board of The Spring, Tampa's domestic violence shelter. In her role as Attorney General, she serves on the Special Olympics Florida Board of Directors and is proud to promote their mission of assisting people with disabilities with being productive and respected members of our communities.

National Association of Drug Diversion Investigators recognized Attorney General Bondi with a 2011 Leadership Award for her efforts to stop prescription drug abuse. In addition, Attorney General Bondi was awarded a special recognition by the Florida Police Chiefs Association for "efforts to reduce prescription drug abuse and strengthen Florida's Prescription Drug Monitoring Program through additional legislation via the 'pill mill' bill."

Additionally, Attorney General Bondi was awarded the Florida Board of Medicine Chairman's Recognition Award for her dedication and service to the people of Florida for her efforts to fight prescription drug abuse.

Attorney General Bondi was awarded the Distinguished Alumna Award in 2011 by Stetson University for extraordinary service to Stetson Law and to the legal profession. During her career as a prosecutor, Attorney General Bondi was awarded the Lawyers of Distinction Award by the Tampa Bay Review for outstanding performance.

Attorney General Bondi is a graduate of University of Florida and Stetson Law School, and has served as a prosecutor for more than 18 years. As an assistant state attorney for the 13th judicial district, her investigative and courtroom experience includes the successful prosecution of numerous first-degree murder cases and two capital cases.

Chief Financial Officer Jeff Atwater

Office Location:
Office of the Chief Financial Officer
Plaza Level 11, The Capitol
Tallahassee, Florida 32399
(850) 413-3100

Mailing:
Office of the Chief Financial Officer
Florida Department of Financial Services
200 East Gaines Street
Tallahassee, FL 32399-0301

Email: Jeff.Atwater@MyFloridaCFO.com

Website: http://www.myfloridacfo.com

Biography

Jeff Atwater serves the citizens of the state of Florida as the state's elected Chief Financial Officer, State Fire Marshal, and as a member of the Florida Cabinet.

A fifth-generation Floridian, husband and father of four, Jeff Atwater was elected Florida's Chief Financial Officer on November 2, 2010, and sworn into office on January 4, 2011. His commitment to public service began in 1993, when his hometown of North Palm Beach elected him Vice Mayor.

Mr. Atwater was subsequently elected to the House of Representatives in 2000 and the Florida Senate in 2002, and was unanimously selected by his fellow senators to serve as Senate President in 2008.

Jeff Atwater's family has had a long and distinguished commitment to public service at local, municipal and state levels. Family values of fairness, stewardship of the public trust, and an unshakeable faith in the American ethos have informed his sense of duty and responsibility in all facets of his public and private careers.

He believes that the principal role of government is to create the conditions where the individuals, families and businesses of Florida are given every opportunity to flourish. Hard work, the value of education, commitment to Judeo-Christian ethics, and belief in the promise of America are to be encouraged and rewarded, not stymied by an over-reaching government.

CFO Atwater's priorities since assuming office have been to aggressively eliminate the fraud that increases the cost of living for Floridians, reduce regulations that inhibit job growth and economic expansion, expand his earlier efforts at fiscal transparency and governmental accountability, and protect the state's most vulnerable citizens from financial harm and abuse.

Mr. Atwater earned his bachelor's degree in finance and an MBA from the University of Florida. His private sector experiences, which included twenty-five years of community banking, provide him a unique and valuable perspective on the sacrifices and challenges facing the business men and women of Florida, as well as the impact of government on the individuals and families of this state.

In addition to his service as an elected official, CFO Atwater has performed volunteer work with many charitable and not-for-profit organizations and has served on a number of governing boards, including the United Way, Chamber of Commerce, Big Brothers and Big Sisters, and Take Stock in Children, among others.

Commissioner of Agriculture Adam H. Putnam

Florida Department of Agriculture and Consumer Services
Plaza Level 10, The Capitol
400 S. Monroe St.
Tallahassee, FL 32399-0800
1-800 HELP-FLA or 1-800-435-7352

Email: Adam.Putnam@FreshFromFlorida.com

Website: http://www.freshfromflorida.com/

Biography

Adam Putnam was elected to serve as Florida's Commissioner of Agriculture on November 2, 2010, and was sworn into office on January 4, 2011. In this capacity, he oversees the Florida Department of Agriculture and Consumer Services, and serves as a member of Florida's Cabinet.

Commissioner Putnam's priorities include fostering the growth and diversification of Florida agriculture; expanding access to Florida's abundance of fresh produce, seafood and other products; securing a stable, reliable and diverse supply of energy; protecting the quantity and quality of the state's water supply; and safeguarding consumers from deceptive business practices.

Commissioner Putnam is also focused on creating opportunities for our nation's wounded veterans to hunt, fish and participate in other outdoor activities on Florida's public lands. More than 300 veterans have enjoyed recreational opportunities on Florida State Forests through Operation Outdoor Freedom, a program of the Florida Forest Service he established in 2011.

Previously, Commissioner Putnam served five terms as Congressman for Florida's 12th Congressional District in the U.S. House of Representatives. He was recognized as a leader on a variety of issues, including water, energy and government transparency and efficiency. Commission Putnam was acknowledged for his efforts to bring comprehensive restoration to the Everglades, reform food safety laws, modernize programs to ensure Florida agriculture remains a leader throughout the nation and increase access to fresh fruits and vegetables to counter childhood obesity.

While in Congress, Commissioner Putnam was elected by his peers to serve as the Republican Policy Chairman during the 109th Congress and Chairman of the House Republican Conference for the 110th Congress, the highest elected leadership position any Floridian of either party has held in Washington. He also served as a member of the House Committees on Government Reform, Agriculture, Rules and Financial Services.

Before he was elected to Congress, Commissioner Putnam served in the Florida House of Representatives from 1996 to 2000. He graduated from the University of Florida with a Bachelor of Science in Food and Resource Economics.

Commissioner Putnam is a fifth generation Floridian who grew up in the citrus and cattle industry. He and his wife, Melissa, have four children.

CHAPTER EIGHT

CONTACT THE DECISION-MAKERS: WHO AND HOW?

THE FLORIDA COMMISSION ON OFFENDER REVIEW

The Florida Commission on Offender Review
4070 Esplanade Way
Tallahassee, FL 32399-2450
Attn: Commission Clerk
Toll Free (855) 850-8196 – or (850) 487-3259
FAX: (850) 921-8712

In addition to directly making parole decisions as described in Chapter 4, the Commission investigates all clemency cases and makes an advisory recommendation to the Board of Executive Clemency.

If you are unable or choose not to attend a parole hearing, you may submit a written statement expressing your support of an inmate, which will be reviewed and considered by the voting commissioners.

First, please review the following, then send an email to:
InmatesSupporter@fcor.state.fl.us

Upon receipt of your email, Commission staff will route your correspondence to the inmate's file for the commissioners' review and consideration. PLEASE NOTE: You will not receive a written response to your e-mail submission.

The inmate's name and Department of Correction's number MUST be included in all correspondence. The **inmate's hearing date should be included**, if known.

The inmate support email address (the one you use to send your comments) is to be used only to express support of an inmate's possible release by the Commission on Offender Review.

The email address should not be used for any other inmate-related inquiries such as their location, inmate banking or visitation procedures, or an inmate's status during the revocation process.

Florida Crime Victim's Bill of Rights
Florida Constitutional Amendment, Article I

Victims of crime or their lawful representatives, including the next of kin of homicide victims, are entitled to be informed, present, and heard, when relevant, at all crucial stages of criminal proceedings, to the extent that these rights do not interfere with the constitutional rights of the accused.

FLORIDA COMMISSION ON OFFENDER REVIEW
(formerly Florida Parole Commission)

COMMISSIONER BIOGRAPHIES

Commissioner Tena M. Pate, Chair, initiated her career in criminal justice in 1979 with the Office of State Attorney for the First Judicial Circuit, and later became the first person appointed to serve as Victims' Advocate for Okaloosa and Walton Counties.

Commissioner Pate relocated to Tallahassee in 1989 to accept a position in the Executive Office of the Governor. In 1993, she accepted the appointment as Florida's Victims' Rights Coordinator in the administration of Governor Lawton Chiles. While in the governor's office, she also served as a Clemency Assistant and State Attorney Liaison for three governors until her appointment to the Florida Parole Commission in 2003 by Governor Bush to fill a vacancy.

On June 24, 2004, Commissioner Pate was appointed to a full six-year term ending June 2010. In 2010 and 2011, she was reappointed by Governors Crist and Scott and the Florida Cabinet for a full six-year term ending June 30, 2016. On August 19, 2014, she was reappointed to serve her third two-year term as Chair by Governor Rick Scott and members of the cabinet. Commissioner Pate has over 30 years of experience working in criminal justice and government relations, and is a member of the Association of Paroling Authorities, Florida Council on Crime and Delinquency, Florida Police Chiefs Association, Leadership Florida and a graduate of the Florida Department of Law Enforcement Chief Executive Seminar.

Commissioner Melinda N. Coonrod, Vice Chair, began her criminal justice career in 1992 when she was appointed to serve as an Assistant State Attorney for the Second Judicial Circuit. As a prosecutor with the State Attorney's Office, she handled a diverse set of criminal cases. She was the lead prosecutor in more than 57 jury trials and more than 30 non-jury trials. During her career as a prosecutor, Commissioner Coonrod gained extensive criminal law experience, and became well-versed in the Florida criminal justice system. She prosecuted perpetrators of crimes, advocated sentencing of those found guilty and worked closely with victims and various law enforcement agencies.

Commissioner Coonrod later served as an Administrative Hearing Officer with the Florida Department of Agriculture and Consumer Services Division of Licensing where she presided over 1400 hearings involving the denial, suspension and revocation of licensure under Chapters 493 and 790, Florida Statutes.

Her experience also includes representing children before the courts as a certified court appointed Guardian Ad Litem, providing training seminars to various law enforcement agencies, and teaching graduate and undergraduate courses as an adjunct instructor at Florida State University College of Criminology and Criminal Justice.

On June 26, 2012, Commissioner Coonrod was appointed by the governor and cabinet to serve on the Commission. On April 29, 2013, she was unanimously confirmed by the Florida Senate to serve a six-year term, which expires June 30, 2018.

On September 19, 2014, the governor and cabinet appointed Commissioner Coonrod to serve a two-year term as Vice Chair of the Commission.

Commissioner Richard D. Davison, Secretary, began his criminal justice career in 1989 as an Assistant State Attorney in the Ninth Judicial Circuit where he prosecuted juvenile delinquency, misdemeanor, and traffic cases in jury and nonjury trials.

In 1991, he became the staff attorney for the Florida House of Representatives Committee on Criminal Justice. He then served as an Assistant Statewide Prosecutor for Florida's Office of Statewide Prosecution where he prosecuted white collar crime, organized crime and other criminal enterprises.

Following the creation of the Florida Department of Juvenile Justice in 1994, Commissioner Davison served as that Department's Director of Legislative Affairs, Assistant General Counsel, and Deputy Secretary. Subsequently, he was appointed Deputy Secretary of the Florida Department of Corrections.

Prior to his appointment to the Commission, Commissioner Davison served as Legal Counsel and Director of Administration for the Gadsden County Sheriff's Office as well as program coordinator for the City of Tallahassee Community Corrections Restorative Justice Program.

He received a Bachelor of Science degree from the Florida State University in 1984, and a Doctor of Jurisprudence from the University of Florida in 1988.

Commissioner Davison was appointed by Governor Scott and the cabinet on August 19, 2014, to serve a six-year term that extends until June 30, 2020. His appointment is subject to confirmation by the Florida Senate.

CHAPTER NINE

ESCAPE – BAD IDEA, DON'T TRY IT!

As you've been reading, this book is about four ways to leave prison early – **LEGALLY!** However, because there recently have been high profile and creative escape attempts, it bears repeating: **Escape is a really bad idea, so don't try it. Period!**

Since the primary audiences for this book are the inmates, their families and supporters, please consider the following:

1. Attempted and actual escapes are illegal.

2. They rarely work.

3. Even a planned or attempted escape, no matter how poorly done, is a NEW CRIME – a second degree felony punishable up to 15 years of ADDITIONAL prison time.

4. The inmate can die or become seriously wounded trying to escape. In addition, they endanger the lives of other inmates, correctional officers, medical personnel, vendors, authorized visitors, civilians, and anyone else close by when the escape is attempted. Or when the FDOC or law enforcement agencies execute the inmate's recapture.

5. In addition to committing a new felony, the inmate will get a very serious disciplinary report, be subject to administrative confinement, and lose numerous privileges like desirable work assignments, gain time and program opportunities.

Remembering the 2003 murder of prison correctional Officer Darla Lathrem illustrates the dangers of attempted escapes.

Officer Lathrem, age 38, was murdered in Charlotte C.I. in Punta Gorda, Florida during an attempted escape by several violent felons, including two convicted killers.

According to FDOC's website, a section entitled Escape Report Summary for Fiscal Year 2012–2013 reported:

- There has not been an escape from the secure perimeter of a major prison since April 2005.

- The majority (94.7%) of the following escapes were community custody "walk-aways" from work release centers, where inmates are out in the community working during the day, returning to the work release center afterward. Inmates returning late from work without valid reasons may be charged with escape and returned to a major prison with a secure perimeter to complete their sentences.

- The remaining escapes in FY 2012–13 were inmates who were working on unarmed work squads outside the perimeter of a prison, and were also inmates under lower levels of custody security.

- In FY 2012–13, there were 172 completed escapes, 170 or 99% of which were recaptured as of July 1, 2013. Of the 170 who were recaptured, 114 or 67% were recaptured within 24 hours of their escape.

- Of the 172 completed escapes, 163 (94.7%) were from non-secure work release/contract centers; five or 2.9% were from a work camp/road prison; and four or 2.4% of the inmates who escaped were housed in prison but were on an outside work detail when they escaped.

- There were seven attempted (and thwarted) escapes in 2012–13.

Escapes by Quarter for FY 2012-13 by Facility Type

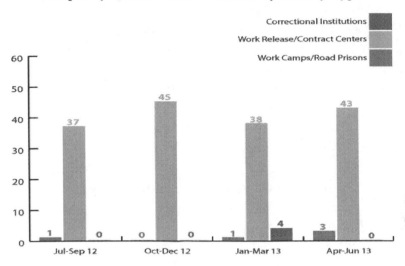

Escapes Over a Ten Year Period*

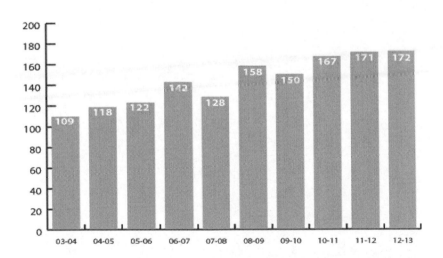

*A majority of escapes are walk-aways from Work Release Centers

The FDOC utilizes three factors to ensure public safety, and maintain a low number of escapes from inside prisons: 1) A zero tolerance policy for escapes; 2) the implementation of a comprehensive security audit program; and 3) replacing and upgrading perimeter barriers including fences, razor wire, and installing electronic detection systems.

Florida's most notorious prison escapee is inmate Mark DeFriest who's had seven successful escapes and six more attempted escapes. DeFriest is a Gadsden County native who initially was sentenced to a four-year term for taking his late father's tools before the will was officially probated.

New York film-maker Gabriel London filmed a documentary called *The Life and Mind of Mark DeFriest*. Though DeFriest is still incarcerated, he continues to pursue a parole release.

Therefore, it bears repeating once again: **It's a really bad idea to attempt an escape, so don't try it. Period!**

CHAPTER TEN

DEAF AND INNOCENT—
FLORIDA INMATE FELIX GARCIA

1981 Tampa Murder Case Screams for Justice

This book has taught you about clemency and parole in Florida. At this time of writing, we are trying both avenues to get Felix Garcia (who is deaf and innocent of the crimes for which he was charged and convicted) out of prison early.

During Felix's November 2014 parole hearing, his presumptive parole release date (PPRD) was set for 2025 when he will be 64 years old. However, this date is not a guaranteed release date as it can be adjusted to an earlier or later release date by the Florida Commission on Offender Review during its next review of his case in August 2017. Felix's team was grateful that he was referred for special programming at Wakulla C.I. near Tallahassee, Florida.

Felix Garcia is a 53-year-old deaf man currently **serving a life sentence** for a **crime he did not commit**, following a 1983 trial during which he could not understand the proceedings and was not provided with a sign language interpreter.

Felix was **framed** for the murder by his older brother, Frank, and his older sister Tina and her boyfriend/pimp Ray Stanley. Felix knew nothing about the murder. But the day after it occurred, Frank asked him to sign a pawn shop ticket for a ring stolen from the murder victim, Joseph Tramontana, Jr.

The pawn shop ticket **was the only physical evidence** on which Felix was convicted of first degree murder and armed robbery.

Felix Garcia has served **approximately 33 years in prison for a murder he did not commit!**

Felix's Seven-Hour Alibi the Night of the Murder

At the time of the murder, Felix was with Michelle Genco (his girlfriend and the mother of his six-month old daughter, Candise Tomorelli).

He was living with his grandmother, Limpado Ahedo, at 203 South Westland Avenue, Tampa, Florida 33606, which was next door to Tina and Ray's apartment. Since Felix did not own a car, Tina, Ray and Frank drove him to see Michelle at the home of her mother, Minerva Genco, at 2517 West Minnehaha Avenue, Tampa, Florida 33614, which was **5.8 miles from the Quality Inn where the murder occurred, at 210 East Fowler Avenue, Tampa, Florida 33612** (now a Rodeway Inn).

A timeline of Felix's activities that evening is as follows:

- **6:30 p.m. (August 3, 1981):** Felix arrived at the home of his girlfriend, Michelle, and her mother, Minerva, located at 2517 West Minnehaha Avenue, Tampa, Florida 33614. Felix had started to walk there, but Tina, Ray and Frank picked him up and gave him a ride.

- **7:22 p.m.:** Domino's Pizza delivery man, Bernie Greenstein, arrived with a pizza at the home of Minerva and Michelle Genco. Felix signed a delivery receipt for the pizza.

- **9:00 p.m.:** Felix saw Carla Genco, Michelle's sister, and Carla's boyfriend, Kent Rosa, at Michelle's home.

- **10:30 p.m.:** After she got off work, Michelle's mother, Minerva, arrived home and was annoyed that Felix was still there. Minerva and Michelle discussed which movie to watch, *The Godfather* or *Motel Hell*, which, per Minerva's *TV Guide*, were both shown that night at the same time and **only** on that particular day. They watched *The Godfather*.

- **1:30 a.m. (August 4, 1981):** A United Cab driver arrived at Michelle's and Minerva's home to pick Felix up and took him back to his home.

Figure 1: Map of Route from Minerva's Home to the Quality Inn

The state prosecutor stated at Felix's 1983 trial that the murder occurred between 8:15 p.m. and 11:00 p.m.

NOTE: As Felix's lead pro bono parole and clemency lawyer, it took me 20 minutes to drive from the "alibi house" to the hotel. Again, Felix did not have a car, much less the time to be in both places at the same time.

Despite Frank's confession in Circuit Court in 2006, and Frank's two affidavits stating that Felix was innocent, **Felix continues to serve a life sentence**.

Felix's avid supporter, retired paralegal Ms. Pat Bliss, and his attorneys and media advocates are currently working pro bono on his case.

Felix Garcia, an innocent inmate, with Pat Bliss, who has worked on his case pro bono for more than 18 years

Felix's Story

Felix Garcia was born in 1961. He grew up with one sister and four brothers. Tina, the eldest, was followed by Frank and then Felix.

When he was three years old, Felix developed a serious ear infection responsible for his eventual hearing loss. It wasn't obvious to Frank or any family member that he had a problem,[50] so he believed he was normal. But his deafness would later result in a fundamentally unfair 1983 trial leading to Felix's approximately 33 years of incarceration for a **crime he did not commit**.

The 1981 Murder of Joseph Tramontana, Jr. in Tampa, Florida

On August 3, 1981, Joseph Tramontana, Jr., age 32, was murdered between 10:00 p.m. and 11:00 p.m. by a single gunshot to the head in his hotel room (number 155) at a Quality Inn in North Tampa at 210 East Fowler Avenue.

Felix's brother, Frank, and his sister Tina's boyfriend, Ray Stanley, had conspired to commit a robbery after estimating the victim's jewelry collection could provide quick cash. Unfortunately, the robbery ultimately led to Tramontana's murder.

Thirteen (13) of Frank's fingerprints were found in the hotel room following the murder.

On August 4, 1981, Frank, Tina and Ray took Felix to a pawnshop and gave him a ring to pawn. Felix did not know where the ring came from. Saying he didn't have any photo identification with him, Frank asked Felix to sign the pawn ticket. Felix still wasn't told where the ring came from, so he didn't know it belonged to the deceased, Joseph Tramontana.[51]

On August 10, 1981, seven days after the murder, Ray was brought to the sheriff's office for questioning. Upon learning he could be a murder suspect, Ray said that Frank and Felix had committed the crime.[52] Frank and Felix were immediately arrested for the murder and robbery of Joseph Tramontana.

Felix's 1983 Trial

Frank was tried and convicted at his trial in 1982. During Felix's trial in 1983, his girlfriend, Michelle, and her mother, Minerva, testified that he was with them during the time of the killing. The pizza delivery receipt Felix signed at 7:22 p.m. at Minerva's house was entered into evidence.

Felix's sister, Tina, and her boyfriend, Ray, both testified for the prosecution that Frank and Felix were the only two people involved. They falsely stated that Felix had told them he shot Mr. Tramontana.

(It's important to note that Ray forced Tina to marry him only eight days after the murder so she would not be compelled to testify against him if he was charged. The law calls this "spousal immunity.")

When Frank was called as a state witness against Felix, he invoked his Fifth Amendment right against self-incrimination and did not testify.

The motives for Frank, Tina and Ray to lie and implicate Felix are now very clear.

Frank blamed Felix to avoid the death penalty. He was successful as he is serving 99 years for second degree murder even though thirteen (13) of his fingerprints were in the hotel room.

Tina accused Felix because Ray Stanley threatened to kill her if she didn't do so (Ray was age 40 and Tina's pimp). Tina, on probation for prostitution, was never charged. Ray accused Frank and Felix to avoid being charged with the armed robbery and murder in which he participated. Ray was never charged, and died on June 18, 1994.

Figure 2: Mug shots of Felix, left (who is innocent), and his brother Frank, right (who is guilty), show how their similar looks and identities could have been confused.

Felix's severe hearing impairment was not adequately addressed, resulting in a fundamentally unfair trial in 1983. The court issued Felix a hearing aid and a loudspeaker, neither of which helped Felix to discern or understand the proceedings.

Due to his hearing loss Felix had only a **fourth grade level** of reading comprehension and listening skills; [53] therefore, he had difficulty understanding legal proceedings during the trial. Felix answered "yes" to questions asked of him, later explaining, "If I say no, they're going to think I'm stupid, will keep repeating the questions. I just wanted to get off the stand and go home."

In July 1983, Felix was convicted of first degree murder and armed robbery on the basis of only one piece of physical evidence (the signed pawn ticket) and Tina and Ray's incriminating testimonies.

Felix received a life sentence for first degree murder, and 99 years for armed robbery.

Life After Felix's Conviction – No Family Support

Felix and his girlfriend, Michelle, parted ways following his conviction, and he never saw her again. Michelle died on December 7, 2013. He has not seen his daughter, Candise, since August of 2012. His mother visited a few times at the beginning of his life sentence. He received a letter years later from his parents saying he was not to look for them if he was ever released.

Felix's younger siblings have not been supportive. They were quite young at the time of the murder, and really didn't know their older brother.

After testifying against Felix in the 1983 trial that put him in prison for life, Tina went on with her life, remarried, and is now a grandmother living in St. Petersburg, Florida. She has written to Felix many times, but has never offered to testify in court to set the record straight. Tina wrote a truthful 1996 affidavit saying Felix was innocent (described below).

In 1996, Pat Bliss (you saw her photo with Felix earlier) – a now-retired paralegal living in Virginia – found evidence that Felix was innocent, and has been working tirelessly on his case for his freedom ever since.

In a letter to Pat in December of 2013, Felix stated...

"Deep inside there is this little kid from when my mom sent me to live with my grandparents. I knew they were leaving me. The image haunts me. I am standing at the door that day and they are leaving and I am crying. I am 52 years old but I feel like a scared kid all over again. All I want is a chance...hope of one day of getting out..."

The Truth Emerges: Frank's and Tina's Subsequent Admissions (1989 to 2006)

Frank's guilty conscience eventually caused him to change his story and tell the truth. In 1989, he provided a written statement, under penalty of perjury, declaring himself the shooter and completely exonerating Felix.[54]

In 1996, Frank made another written statement, this time stating Ray did the shooting, and that Felix was not present at the crime. At the end of this second statement, Frank again emphatically stated that Felix was innocent and had nothing to do with the crime.[55]

Also in 1996, Tina signed a similar affidavit under oath stating that Felix was innocent and had nothing to do with the crime.[56] She likely felt compelled to offer her truthful statement after Ray's death in 1994, when he was no longer a threat to her safety.

In 2006, Felix was given an evidentiary hearing in circuit court in Tampa, Florida, based on newly-discovered evidence that he was innocent. Frank was initially called by the defense to verify that he had told fellow inmates he was responsible for putting his innocent deaf brother in prison for a crime he did not commit.

Frank then confessed to the murder in open court, and admitted that in his 1982 trial testimony he had lied to the jury and his attorney by first pointing the finger at Felix as the shooter[57], and later stating that both Ray and Felix did the shooting.[58]

However, the judge – uncertain of what or whom to believe – refused to free Felix and denied his motion for a new trial.

In 2010, Frank wrote his brother a letter, in which he stated,

"I did the best I could to make a wrong that I did right for you. You don't understand the pain in my heart, because I am to blame for us doing 30 years so far in prison." [59]

Since 1989, Frank has tried repeatedly to reverse the wrong he committed against his brother Felix, going so far as to state in the 2006 evidentiary hearing that he has tried to exonerate Felix since his trial,[60] but to no avail.

Model Inmate Felix Garcia's Prison Accomplishments

The facts about Felix Garcia's seven-hour alibi and total innocence probably leaves you asking yourself, *How can he have served 33 years in state prison, especially after his brother and sister stated under oath that Felix is totally innocent?* The answer is the criminal justice system isn't perfect.

Yet, Felix knows he is innocent! His volunteer paralegal of 18 years, Ms. Pat Bliss, knows he is innocent! His entire team of pro-bono lawyers, advocates and media advisors believe he is innocent! I have interviewed him twice during a six-month period, and **I also believe he is innocent!**

While we continue to work to free Felix Garcia through clemency or parole, please:

- Look below at his amazing prison resume as a model inmate and mentor to other inmates.

- Visit his website, www.FreeFelix Now.com, to see a short three-minute video of his case, and to keep up with recent developments.

- Join more than 106,000 people who support Felix's release by going to www.change.org to sign a petition!

FELIX GARCIA'S PRISON RESUME

Work Experience and Vocational Education:
Horizon Character-Based Transition Program and Others

- Development of website for Horizon Character-Based Transition Program (2014)

- Certificate of Accomplishment Mavis Beacon Typing Institute (July 2014)

- Certificate of Recognition on Microsoft Access (July 2014)

- Certificate of Achievement AutoCAD 2000 (April–June 2014)

- Horizon Character-Based Transition Program: Certificate of Recognition for Completion of Microsoft Interactive Windows XP, Office Word, and Office Word Advanced (2013)

- Horizon Character-Based Transition Program: Certificate of Completion of AutoCAD 2000 (2013)

- Horizon Character-Based Transition Program: Certificate of Completion of AutoCAD 2000: Instructor (2013)

- Certificate of Completion: Certified Law Clerk (2013)

- National Center For Construction Education Certificates in: (2010)

  o Sprinkler Fitting Level One

  o Pipe Trade Technology V36

- State Certificate for Occupational Competency: Fire Sprinkler Installer 2 (2010)

- National Center For Construction Education completion in training in 14 areas of construction including COVC Pipe and Fittings, Copper Tube Systems, Underground Pipe, Steel Pipe, Basic Rigging, Introduction to Blueprints, Hand Tools and Power Tools (2010)

- Certificate of Satisfactorily Completed Occupational Competencies in Plumber-0646050302 (2008)

- Outstanding Assistance In Setting Up The Student Records Database for Sheet Metal Fabrication Technology (2000)

- Certificate of Completion in General Office Clerk for Employability, Functions, Office Practices, Keyboarding, Information Processing, Basic, Filing, and Purchasing and Receiving (1996)

- Certificate of Completion in CAD Operator for DOS System, Employability, Basic, Computer Operator (1996)

- Business Technical Institute course (1993)

- Data Entry Business Application Diploma, Branell Institute (1992)

- Prepared booklet on computer printing processes for Florida Department of State, Bureau of Florida Folklore Programs (1990)

- Certificate of Training in Pressman (1990)

- GED earned while in prison (1984)

Education and Life Skills:
Horizon Character-Based Transition Program

- Certificate of Completion Advanced Art Class (July 2014)

- Certificate of Completion for Diabetes Awareness Course (July 2014)

- Certificate of Graduation for REEFs Personal Finance (June 2014)

- Certificate of Graduation for Pathways to Sobriety (May 2014)

- Participant of the Month for Valuable Service to Horizon Character-Based Community (2013 and 2014)

- Parole Planning Workshop (2013)

- Certificate of Completion in Anger Management in the Horizon Character-Based Transition Program (2013)

- Certificate of Recognition for Completion of "17 Laws of Team Leadership" in the Horizon Character-Based Transition Program (2013)

- Certificate for Completing Elective Class "How We Shall Live" in Horizon Character-Based Program (2013)

- Joined Unlimited Gavel Club, an affiliate of Toastmasters International (2011 and 2012)

- Unlimited Gavel Club "Best Speaker" (January 2012) meeting for a speech-on-speech impairment for Health Awareness Month.

- Outstanding Library Participant in the Legal Education Seminar (2012)

- Certificate of Award for Contribution to Health Awareness Month (2012)

- Certificate of Achievement in Anger Resolution Seminar (2005 & 2010)

- Certificates of Loyal Service for Six Years to PRIDE Enterprises at Polk CI. (2000)

- Certificate of Completion for 1996 Year of Awareness Workshop (1996)

- Completed training module in Basic Safety Orientation (1996)

Faith-Based Achievements

- In pursuit of his faith, Felix completed numerous Bible Correspondence Courses, including (2012):

  o American Bible Academy (Two courses)

  o Airport Road Church of Christ (Two courses)

  o Center for Evangelism and Discipleship/Global University (Five courses)

  o Lamp and Light Bible Course (One course)

  o Set Free Ministries (Nine courses)

  o Wisconsin Evangelist Lutheran Synod/Prison Ministry Committee (Five courses)

  o World Bible School (Four courses)

- Thirty-one additional faith-based courses in 2011

- Baptized in December 2011

CHAPTER ELEVEN

CALL TO ACTION!
GET STARTED NOW

You now have the "how-to" steps and knowledge to act on your own or with a lawyer. Next, you should take these three steps:

1. Complete and submit the following brief form, then either:

   - email it to reggie@floridaclemencylawyer.com
   - mail it to P.O. Box 11069, Tallahassee, FL 32302, or
   - fax it to 850-222-3957

   Once it's received, you are eligible to get free updates of this book; future legal articles; and Reggie's blog posts about changes in Florida law.

2. Submit the following information form. Or contact the author (Reggie Garcia) to request a telephone conference regarding the information contained in this book.

3. Help an inmate prepare his or her prison resume (use Felix Garcia's sample prison resume in Chapter 10 as a "how-to" guide)

Inmate's Information

Name: _____

D.C. Number _____

Date of Birth _____

Relative's or Supporter's Contact Information:

Name: _____

Home phone: _____

Cell phone: _____

Address: _____

Email Address: _____

ABOUT THE AUTHOR

Reggie Garcia, Esq., is an AV Preeminent®-rated attorney by Martindale-Hubbell, achieving the rating agency's **highest marks** for both competency and ethics. He also is an experienced state government lobbyist.

Described by the media as an "expert in clemency and parole cases," he has visited 29 state prisons. He is a frequent public speaker, and has appeared on national network and cable TV news programs, on Florida broadcast affiliate TV stations, on the radio and published in legal magazines and newspapers.

Reggie graduated in 1982 from the University of Florida College of Journalism and Communications, and in 1985 from the University of Florida Levin College of Law where he was the president of the leadership honorary society Florida Blue Key.

A Tampa native, he resides in Tallahassee, Florida.

Connect with Reggie Garcia:

Email:	reggie@floridaclemencylawyer.com
Web:	www.FloridaClemencyLawyer.com
Facebook:	facebook.com/reggiegarcia
Twitter:	@clemencylawyer
Address:	P.O. Box 11069, Tallahassee, FL 32302
Fax:	850-222-3957

APPENDIX A

Commutation of Sentence Cases Granted 1980 to Present

Commutation of Sentence Cases Granted 1980 Through December 31, 2013

Governor Bob Graham (1979-1987)

LAST	FIRST	MID	SUF	OFFENSE	SENTENCE	GRANTED DATE	BOARD ACTION	ID
MAGNANI	Paul			1st Degree Murder	25 years mandatory	6/12/1980	COS from life to 25 years	1
WASHINGTON	Willie			Aggravated Battery	3 years mandatory	7/8/1981	COS to time served	2
GLANDER	Robert	J.		Introduction of Contraband into Prison	3 years	8/4/1981	COS to time served	3
MORRIS	Exa	Bell		1st Degree Murder	25 years mandatory	3/11/1982	COS to time served	4
PURVIS	Michael			Aggravated Assault	3 years mandatory	6/15/1982	COS – remove mandatory	5
BARREDO	Mary			1st Degree Murder	25 years mandatory	9/15/1982	COS – remove mandatory	6
D'ANDREA	Carolyn			Drug Trafficking	5 years mandatory	5/18/1983	COS – remove mandatory	7
WILLIS	Albert			Burglary; Grand Theft; Escape	3 years mandatory	6/15/1983	COS to time served	8
STRINGER	George			Aggravated Assault	3 years mandatory	6/21/1983	COS – remove mandatory	9
PIERCE	Abraham			Drug Trafficking	15 years mandatory	12/14/1983	COS – remove mandatory	10
SUTTILE	Nicholas			Drug Trafficking	5 years mandatory	1/19/1984	COS – remove mandatory	11
LEIGH	Ronald	Fay		1st Degree Murder	25 years mandatory	3/21/1984	COS – remove mandatory	12
ABELLA	Irene			1st Degree Murder	25 years mandatory	7/24/1984	COS – remove mandatory	13
MANNING	David	Earl		1st Degree Murder	25 years mandatory	3/13/1985	COS – remove mandatory	14
MORGAN	Dean	Ross		1st Degree Murder	25 years mandatory	5/7/1985	COS – remove mandatory	15
ALLEN	Ina	Louise		Aggravated Battery	30 months	8/20/1985	COS to time served	16
LEE	Ruby			1st Degree Murder	25 years mandatory	12/18/1985	COS – remove mandatory	17
RAFFONE	James	Louis		Drug Trafficking	5 years mandatory	11/6/1986	COS – remove mandatory	18
HESSE	Frank			Drug Trafficking	5 years mandatory	12/5/1986	COS – remove mandatory	19
COLLINS	Horace	D.		Lewd & Lascivious	7 years	12/19/1986	COS to time served	20
DEESE	William	J.		1st Degree Murder	25 years mandatory	12/19/1986	COS - remove mandatory	21

Governor Bob Martinez (1987-1991)

LAST	FIRST	MID	SUF	OFFENSE	SENTENCE	GRANTED DATE	BOARD ACTION	ID
MURDOCK	Dennis			DUI Manslaughter	19 years	3/10/1987	COS to time served, Revoked 4/10/87	22
COLLINS	Carl			Aggravated Assault	3 years mandatory	12/3/1987	COS – remove mandatory	23
DELGROSSO	Joseph			Drug Trafficking	5 years mandatory	12/3/1987	COS – remove mandatory	24
STINSON	Benson			Drug Trafficking	5 years mandatory	12/3/1987	COS – remove mandatory	25
LEWELLYN	David			Burglary, Gr. Theft	13 years	3/23/1988	COS to time served	26
LOPEZ	Ada			1st Degree Murder	25 years mandatory	3/23/1988	COS – remove mandatory	27
MATTINGLY	Thomas			1st Degree Murder	25 years mandatory	3/23/1988	COS – remove mandatory	28
SHAPIRO	William			1st Degree Murder	25 years mandatory	3/23/1988	COS – time served	29

LAST	FIRST	MID	SUF	OFFENSE	SENTENCE	GRANTED DATE	BOARD ACTION	ID
ANDREWS	Joan			Burglary/Arson	5 years	10/14/1988	COS – time served	30
JAMES	Michael			Robbery/Burglary	9 years	4/12/1989	COS – time served	31
PERRY	Eddie	Mae		Aggr. Assault	3 years mandatory	4/12/1989	COS – time served	32
STARK	Thomas	H.		Aggr. Assault	3 years mandatory	12/6/1989	COS – time served	33
GARCIA	Hermes			Trafficking Cocaine	15 years mandatory	12/6/1989	COS – time served	34
WUCHTE	Mark	L.		Aggr. Assault	3 years mandatory	12/21/1989	COS – time served	35
GILBERT	Roswell			1st Degree Murder	25 years mandatory	8/1/1990	COS – time served	36
WILLIS	Fran			1st Degree Murder	25 years mandatory	12/19/1990	COS – time served	37

Governor Lawton Chiles (1991-1998)

LAST	FIRST	MID	SUF	OFFENSE	SENTENCE	GRANTED DATE	BOARD ACTION	ID
DEBARR	Jean			1st Degree Murder	25 years mandatory	9/24/1991	COS – time served	38
HERMAN	Mark			1st Degree Murder	25 years mandatory	1/31/1992	COS – time served	39
LYONS	Tanya			1st Degree Murder	25 years mandatory	3/12/1992	COS – mandatory portion, removed	40
TAYLOR	Jerry	Merrill		1st Degree Murder	25 years mandatory	8/18/1992	COS – time served	41
SCOTT	Artemus			Aggr. Battery	3 years mandatory	12/8/1992	COS – mandatory removed	42
STONE	Troy			1st Degree Murder	25 years mandatory	12/8/1992	COS – mandatory removed	43
SOUBIELLE	Kimberly	B.		2nd Degree Murder	30 years	3/10/1993	COS – time served	44
MATHIS	Sylvester			1st Degree Murder	25 years mandatory	3/10/1993	COS – mandatory removed	45
MAUGERI	Joseph			1st Degree Murder	25 years mandatory	3/10/1993	COS – time served	46
PEOPLES	Sylvester			1st Degree Murder	25 years mandatory	6/9/1993	COS – mandatory removed	47
RILEY	Accie			1st Degree Murder	25 years mandatory	6/9/1993	COS – mandatory removed	48
RAINES	Billie	Jean		1st Degree Murder	25 years mandatory	7/14/1993	COS – time served	49
DIXON	Donald			1st Degree Murder	25 years mandatory	9/1/1993	COS – mandatory removed	50
GRAY	Daniel	E.		1st Degree Murder	25 years mandatory	9/1/1993	COS – mandatory removed	51
RENFROE	Wayne			Sale of Cocaine	3 years mandatory	9/1/1993	COS – mandatory removed	52
BURT	Shalanda			2nd Degree Murder	17 years	10/26/1993	COS – reduced to 7 years, Revoked – 4/17/96	53
HAETTICH	Arthur			1st Degree Murder	25 years mandatory	10/26/1993	COS – removed mandatory	54
PALMER	Angelo			1st Degree Murder	25 years mandatory	11/23/1993	COS – removed mandatory	55
OSORIO	Alejandro			1st Degree Murder	25 years mandatory	12/7/1993	COS – time served	56
COLLIGAN	John	C.		Battery on LEO	3 year mandatory	12/7/1993	COS – removed mandoaty	57
TOMLINSON	Robert	W.		2nd Degree Murder	20 years	12/16/1993	COS – reduced sentence to 11 years, Revoked 6/4/97	58
CARRIZALES	Martin			1st Degree Murder	25 years mandatory	6/8/1994	COS – reduced 25 year mandatory to 20 years	59

LAST	FIRST	MID	SUF	OFFENSE	SENTENCE	GRANTED DATE	BOARD ACTION	ID
FLETCHER	Sherman			Aggr. Assault	3 years mandatory	6/14/1994	COS – time served	60
CLUGSTON	Christopher			1st Degree Murder	25 years mandatory	7/22/1994	COS – time served	61
ALFONSO	Henry			Drug Trafficking	15 years mandatory	12/14/1994	COS – time served	62
RAMIREZ	Rafael			Drug Trafficking	15 years mandatory	12/14/1994	COS – time served	63
REGISTER	Johnny			1st Degree Murder	25 years mandatory	12/14/1994	COS – removed mandatory	64
SCHREMMER	Herbert			Drug Trafficking	15 years mandatory	12/14/1994	COS – time served	65
SIMMONS	Clarence			Drug Trafficking	15 years mandatory	12/14/1994	COS – time served	66
FRENCH	Lisa			2nd Degree Murder	12 years	12/21/1994	COS – time served	67
GELIS	Elizabeth			2nd Degree Murder	22 years	12/21/1994	COS on Count 1 – time served; Count 2 stands	68
KENT	Lynn	H.		2nd Degree Murder	15 years	12/21/1994	COS – time served	69
LAMB	Sheranita			2nd Degree Murder	25 years	12/21/1994	COS – reduced to 15 years, Revoked 1/31/2000	70
LEONBERGER	Maricka			2nd Degree Murder	30 years	12/21/1994	COS – reduced to 15 years	71
RICHMOND	Gordon			1st Degree Murder	25 years mandatory	12/21/1994	COS – reduced 25 years mandatory to 12 years	72
ROBARE	Susan			2nd Degree Murder	15 years	12/21/1994	COS – reduced 15 years to 12 years	73
TRUBILLA	Elec			1st Degree Murder	25 years mandatory	12/21/1994	COS – removed mandatory	74
JOHNSON	Richard			Aggravated Assault	3 years mandatory	12/21/1994	COS – reduced 3 years mandatory to 30 months	75
RICHARDSON	Albert			Aggravated Assault	3 years mandatory	12/21/1994	COS – removed mandatory	76
BRASWELL	Bret			Drug Trafficking	15 years mandatory	12/29/1994	COS – reduced 15 years mandatory to 12 years	77
BROWN	Allison		Jr.	Drug Trafficking	15 years mandatory	12/29/1994	COS – reduced 15 years mandatory to 12 years	78
DEAN	Byron			Drug Trafficking	15 years mandatory	12/21/1994	COS – reduced 15 years mandatory to 12 years	79
HANLEY	John	L.		Drug Trafficking	15 years mandatory	12/21/1994	COS – reduced 15 years mandatory to 12 years	80
O'BARA	Colleen			Burgl/Grand Theft	20 months	3/15/1995	COS – time served	81
BLACKSHEAR	Jerome			Burglary/Robbery/Aggravated Battery	30 years	3/13/1996	COS – time served, Revoked 10/30/96	82
TERHUNE	Dabney			2nd Degree Murder	22 years	4/18/1996	COS – reduced 22 years to 13 years	83
ELDRED	Dwight		Jr.	DUI Manslaughter	8 years	10/16/1996	COS – time served	84
HOWELL	Dianne			2nd Degree Murder	22 years	5/6/1997	COS – reduced 22 years to time served	85
SMITH	Dustin	Keith		Lewd Act on Child	6 years	6/12/1997	COS – time served	86

LAST	FIRST	MID	SUF	OFFENSE	SENTENCE	GRANTED DATE	BOARD ACTION	ID
WILLIAMS	James	Lee		Sexual Battery on a Child	Life/25 Mandatory	6/12/1997	COS – time served	87
THOMAS	Shirley	K.		2nd Degree Murder	22 years followed by 8 years prob.	9/16/1997	COS – reduce 22 year sentence to time served & 8 year prob. to 3 years	88
MEMRO	Helen	C.		2nd Degree Murder	12 years	12/19/1997	COS – time served & 3 years probation	89
NEWSOME	Denise	Y.		1st Degree Murder	Life/25 Mandatory	12/19/1997	COS – Commute mandatory & reduce life to 33 years; 3 yrs. probation	90
ZUBER	Rebecca	Marie		1st Degree Murder	Life/25 Mandatory	12/19/1997	COS – reduced to time served; 3 yrs. probation	91
MERRELL	Douglas			Drug Trafficking	5 years	3/24/1998	COS – time served	92
BRUNO	Michael			Aggravated Assault w/Firearm	3 year mandatory	5/13/1998	COS – time served	93
MOREAU	Randall			DUI/Manslaughter	7 years	6/12/1998	COS – time served	94
GELIS	Elizabeth			2nd Degree Murder	22 years	8/11/1998	COS – reduce 22 year sentence on Ct. 2 to 17 years	95
KERN	Richard	M.		2nd Degree Murder		8/11/1998	COS – time served on Count 3	96
QUICK	Shirley	B.		1st Degree Murder	Life/25 Mandatory	8/11/1998	COS – time served; 3 years probation; Spend one year at residential treatment facility	97
TYLER	Debra	D.		1st Degree Murder		8/11/1998	COS – time served; 3 years probation; Spend one year at residential treatment facility	98
RANDLEY	Loretta			Manslaughter	4 years	9/18/1998	COS – time served	99
GIBSON	Jewel	Dean		2nd Degree Murder	12 years	10/15/1998	COS – time served	100
JACKSON	Katrina	M.		2nd Degree Murder	40 years & 5 years probation	11/5/1998	COS – incarceration portion of sentence to time served; complete 5 year probation; Spend one year at residential treatment facility	101
RICHARDS	Dana	Estes		2nd Degree Murder	18 years & 5 years probation	11/5/1998	COS – incarceration portion of sentence to time served; complete 5 year probation; Spend one year at residential treatment facility	102

Governor Buddy MacKay (1998 and 1999)

LAST	FIRST	MID	SUF	OFFENSE	SENTENCE	GRANTED DATE	BOARD ACTION	ID
DUQUE	Tammy			1st Degree Murder	Life/25 Mandatory	12/23/1998	COS – time served; 3 years probation; Spend one year at residential treatment facility	103

LAST	FIRST	MID	SUF	OFFENSE	SENTENCE	GRANTED DATE	BOARD ACTION	ID
FIELDS	Theresa			2nd Degree Murder	40 years	12/23/1998	COS – time served; 3 years probation; Spend one year at residential treatment facility	104
HART	Deborah	L.		1st Degree Murder	Life/25 Mandatory	12/23/1998	COS – time served; 3 years probation; Spend one year at residential treatment facility	105
LEWIS	Michelle	D.		2nd Degree Murder	20 years	12/23/1998	COS – time served; 3 years probation; Spend one year at residential treatment facility	106
MCKEE	Cheri			1st Degree Murder	Life/25 Mandatory	12/23/1998	COS – time served; 3 years probation; Spend one year at residential treatment facility	107
WEIAND	Kathleen			2nd Degree Murder	18 years	12/23/1998	COS – time served; 3 years probation; Spend one year at residential treatment facility	108
BOWLING	Ted	Randy		Robbery and Kidnapping	40 years	12/23/1998	COS of 1/3 jurisdiction held by court to be parole eligible	109
SCHULER	Anthony			Robbery	20 years	12/23/1998	COS – time served; complete 3 year court ordered probation; Spend one year at residential treatment facility	110
BLAYLOCK	Lawrence			1st Degree Murder	Life/25 Mandatory	1/4/1999	COS – reduced life sentence to 53 years	111
ROGER	Michelle			2nd Degree Murder	17 years	1/4/1999	COS – reduced 17 year sentence to 11 years; 3 years probation; Spend one year at residential treatment facility	112

Governor Jeb Bush (1999-2007)

LAST	FIRST	MID	SUF	OFFENSE	SENTENCE	GRANTED DATE	BOARD ACTION	ID
NEWNHAM	Susan			Obtaining Property by Worthless Check (5 cases)	25 Years	3/23/1999	COS – time served; Spend one year at residential treatment facility	113
BUTT	Casey	Mason		2nd Degree Murder	10 years & 10 years probation	7/9/1999	COS – time served; serve 10 years court-ordered probation; Spend one year at residential treatment facility	114
BRADLEY	Sandra	Hall		Obtaining Property by Worthless Check; Escape; Forgery; Fraudulent Use of Credit Card; Felony Petit Theft	14 years cumulative	7/19/2002	COS – time served; serve court ordered probation, Spend one year at residential treatment facility, Spend one year at residential treatment facility, Revoked 11/25/2003	115

LAST	FIRST	MID	SUF	OFFENSE	SENTENCE	GRANTED DATE	BOARD ACTION	ID
FLEITAS	Juan			1st Degree Murder	w/25 year mandatory	9/26/2003	COS – changed sentence from life to 40 years on each to run concurrent	116
WALLER	Shane	Ritchie		DUI Manslaughter	8 years	9/25/2003	COS – time served; complete court-ordered probation of 22 years successfully; Revoked – 9/20/2005	117
HASLAM	Kimberly			Armed Robbery; Kidnapping; Attempted Murder of Law Officer	40 years	10/6/2003	COS – time served on incarceration portion; must serve 15 years probation and one year at residential treatment facility	118
HIGGINBOTHAM	James	M.		2nd Degree Murder	12 years	6/21/2004	COS – sentence commuted to probation until sentence completed on condition he complete probation successfully	119
GROEN	Darren			2nd Degree Murder	31 years	12/9/2004	COS – sentence commuted on condition he serve remainder of sentence on supervision and complete one year at residential treatment facility	120
DEARRIBA	Alexander			Burglary, Grand Theft	12 years	12/23/2004	COS – incarceration portion commuted to time served; complete court ordered probation and complete one year at residential treatment facility	121
STATH	Jeannette			2nd Degree Murder, Arson of Dwelling	16 years	7/6/2005	COS – incarceration portion commuted to time served; complete court ordered probation and complete one year at residential treatment facility	122
THOMPSON	Megan	Ashley		DUI Manslaughter	3 years 9 mos.	12/6/2005	COS – sentence commuted to time served and placed on probation to terminate 12/11/2011	123
WILSON	Frank	Jr.		Robbery; Kidnapping	39 years	12/6/2005	COS – sentence commuted from life to 39.7 years; upon release to be on 10 years probation	124
SCREWS	Roy	A.	Jr.	Drug Trafficking	30 years	2/22/2006	COS – sentence commuted to time served with supervision and complete one year at residential treatment facility.	125

LAST	FIRST	MID	SUF	OFFENSE	SENTENCE	GRANTED DATE	BOARD ACTION	ID
BLOOM	Casey	M.		DUI Manslaughter	12 years probation	3/28/2006	COS – to time served, (Also granted a full pardon and restoration of civil rights)	126
STANGHERLIN	Jacqueline			2nd Degree Murder	75 years	3/29/2006	COS – sentence commuted from 300 years to 75 years and removal of 150 year jurisdiction of court to make her parole eligible.	127
MCDAVID	Daniel	M.		Grand Theft, Forgery, Uttering	5 years	8/30/2006	COS to time served.	128
CUSHMAN	Scott			DUI Manslaughter	14 years	9/21/2006	COS of incarceration to time served on condition he serve probation until 2012	129
SMITH	Derrick			DUI Manslaughter	10 years	10/27/2006	COS from 10 years to 8 years	130
FANNON	Thomas			Trafficking in Cannabis	Probation	11/8/2006	COS of probation to time served; Remission of Fine	131
RODAMMER	Brandon			Trafficking in GHB	5 years & 6 mos.	12/7/2006	COS to be eligible for release on 12/20/2007	132
PATRIA	Sandra			1st Degree Murder	Life with 25 year mandatory	12/14/2006	COS to time served; 42 mos. probation with 18 mos. at domestic violence facility	133
PERRY	Sherry			1st Degree Murder	Life with 25 year mandatory	12/14/2006	COS to time served; 18 mos. probation to be served at domestic violence facility	134
Governor Charlie Crist (2007-2011)								
PAEY	Richard			Drug Trafficking	25 year mandatory	9/20/2007	COS to time served; Full Pardon; Remission of Fine	135
TANNER	Holly			Drug Trafficking	7 years	12/6/2007	COS to time served on condition she serve one year supervision with random drug testing	136
BARBER	Earle			Burglary/Dealing in Stolen Property	9 years	12/6/2007	COS to time served	137
SANCHEZ	Daniel			Trafficking in Cocaine	Life w/o parole	2/28/2008	COS to time served	138
SAKEMILLER	Jeffrey			DUI Manslaughter	11 years	6/5/2008	COS to time served	139
ANDERSON	Eddie	Joe		DUI Serious Bodily Injury	10 years, 11 mos.	6/5/2008	COS of prison sentence; complete court ordered probation	140

LAST	FIRST	MID	SUF	OFFENSE	SENTENCE	GRANTED DATE	BOARD ACTION	ID
KEEHN	Donald			Shooting At, Within, Or Into A Building (5 Counts)	3 year mandatory	3/12/2009	COS to time served on condition he not return to Florida	141
MARTIN	Jennifer	L.		Manslaughter by Culpable Negligence	192.6 months	12/15/2009	COS to time served	142
ALBRITTON	Virginia			Grand Theft (5 Counts)	8.1 years, followed by 21 years probation	6/3/2010	COS to time served, including probation	143
BUNKLEY	Clyde	Timothy		Armed Burglary	Life	9/23/2010	COS to time served	144
TRAPCHAK	Wesley	Wilson		Armed Robbery	Life	12/9/2010	COS to time served	145
BAKER	Monique	J.		Trafficking in Cocaine	35 years	12/9/2010	COS to time served	146
SQUIRES	Suzanne	Conroy		DUI Manslaughter, DUI Resulting in Serious Bodily Injuries – 3 Counts	277.6 months	12/9/2010	COS to time served	147

Governor Rick Scott (2011-present)

LAST	FIRST	MID	SUF	OFFENSE	SENTENCE	GRANTED DATE	BOARD ACTION	ID
KELLY	Joseph	Francis		Trafficking in Cocaine Conspiracy to Traffic in Cocaine	20 year, with 15 year mandatory	12/12/2013	COS – 15 years prison, followed by 5 years probation	148

APPENDIX B
COMMUNITY RELEASE CENTERS

WORK RELEASE CENTERS
LOCATED IN THREE FLORIDA REGIONS

Region 1

Panama City Community Release Center (Male)
3609 Highway 390
Panama City, Florida 32405-2795
(850) 872-4178 Fax (850) 747-5739

Pensacola Community Release Center (Male)
3050 North L. Street
Pensacola, Florida 32501-1010
(850) 595-8920 Fax (850) 595-8919

SHISA House - West (Female)
(Contract Facility)
418 West Virginia Street
Tallahassee, Florida 32301-1030
(850) 222-4859 Fax (850) 222-8467

Tallahassee Community Release Center (Male)
2616A Springhill Road
Tallahassee, Florida 32305-6739
(850) 488-2478 Fax (850) 922-6240

Region 2

Bridges of Jacksonville (Male)
(Contract facility)
601 Agmac Avenue
Jacksonville, Florida 32254
(904) 674-0850

Bridges of Lake City (Male)
(Contract Facility)
1099 N.W. Dot Court
Lake City, Florida 32055-2564
(386) 628-5130

Bridges of Santa Fe (Male)
(Contract Facility)
2901 Northeast 39th Avenue
Gainesville, Florida 32602-1202
(352) 955-2070

Daytona Beach Community Release Center (Male)
3601 U.S. Highway 92 West
Daytona Beach, Florida 32124-1002
(386) 238-3171 Fax: (386) 947-4058

Jacksonville Bridge (Male)
(Contract facility)
601 Agmac Avenue
Jacksonville, Florida 32254
(904) 674-0850

Re-Entry Center of Ocala (Male)
(Contract facility)
2006 N.E. 8th Road
Ocala, Florida 34470-4231
(352) 351-1280 Fax: (352) 351-8213

SHISA House - East (Female)
(Contract Facility)
2830 Park Street Jacksonville, Florida
32205-8017
(904) 389-1303 Fax (904) 389-1302

Tomoka CRC - 298 (Male)
(Contract Facility)
1341 Indian Lake Road
Daytona Beach, Florida 32124
(386) 236-3308

Tomoka CRC - 285 (Male)
(Contract Facility)
1200 Red John Road
Daytona Beach, Florida 32124
(386) 236-3308

TTH of Dinsmore (Male)
(Contract Facility)
13200 Old Kings Road
Jacksonville, Florida 32219
(904) 999-4220

Region 3

Atlantic Community Release Center (Female)
263 Fairgrounds Road
West Palm Beach, Florida 33411-3639
(561) 791-4187

Bradenton Bridge (Female)
(Contract facility)
2104 63rd Avenue, East
Bradenton, Florida 34203-5012
(941) 932-9030 Fax: (941) 932-9025

Bridges of Cocoa (Male)
(Contract Facility)
585 Camp Road
Cocoa, Florida 32927-4738
(321) 338-4550

Bridges of Orlando (Male)
(Contract facility)
2007 North Mercy Drive
Orlando, Florida 32808-5613
(407) 218-4573

Bridges of Pompano (Male)
(Contract Facility)
400 F SW 2nd Street
Pompano Beach, Florida 33060-6822
(954) 580-0949

Broward Bridge (Male)
(Contract Facility)
5600 Northwest 9th Avenue
Ft. Lauderdale, Florida 33309-2800
(954) 358-2650 Fax: (954) 358-2652

Fort Pierce Community Release Center (Male)
1203 Bell Avenue
Ft. Pierce, Florida 34982-6599
(772) 468-3929 Fax: (772) 467-3140

Hollywood Community Release Center (Female)
8501 W. Cypress Drive
Pembroke Pines, Florida 33025-4542
(954) 985-4720 Fax: (954) 967-1251

Kissimmee Community Release Center (Male)
2925 Michigan Avenue
Kissimmee, Florida 34744-1200
(407) 846-5210 Fax: (407) 846-5368

Miami North Community Release Center (Male)
7090 Northwest 41st Street
Miami, Florida 33166-6817
(305) 470-5580 Fax (305) 470-5584

Opa Locka Community Release Center (Male)
5400 Northwest 135th Street
Opa Locka, Florida 33054-4310
(305) 827-4057 Fax: (305) 364-3188

Orlando Bridge (Male)
(Contract facility)
2025 North Mercy Drive
Orlando, Florida 32808
(407) 218-4575 Fax (407) 218-4591

Orlando Community Release Center (Female)
7300 Laurel Hill Drive
Orlando, Florida 32818-5278
(407) 578-3510 Fax: (407) 578-3509

Pinellas Community Release Center (Female)
5205 Ulmerton Road
Clearwater, Florida 33760-4002
(727) 570-5138 Fax: (727) 570-3187

St. Petersburg Community Release Center (Male)
4237 8th Avenue, South
St. Petersburg, Florida 33711-2000
(727) 893-2289 Fax: (727) 893-1182

Suncoast Community Release Center (Female)
(Contract facility)
10596 Gandy Boulevard
St. Petersburg, Florida 33702-1422
(727) 523-1423 Fax: (727) 578-0241

Tampa Community Release Center (Male)
(Contract Facility)
3630 N. 50th Street
Tampa Florida 33619
(813) 629-2867

TTH of Bartow (Male)
(Contract Facility)
550 N. Restwood Avenue
Bartow, Florida 33830-4200
(863) 733-4181

TTH of Kissimmee (Male)
(Contract facility)
900 East Vine Street
Kissimmee, Florida 34744
(407) 846-0068

TTH of Tarpon Springs (Male)
(Contract Facility)
566 Brady Road
Tarpon Springs, Florida 34689-6707
(727) 940-6936

**West Palm Beach Community
Release Center (Male)**
261 West Fairgrounds Road
West Palm Beach, FL 33411-3639
(561) 791-4750
Fax: (561) 791-4018

APPENDIX C

APPROVED TRANSITIONAL HOUSING LIST

Care of Tallahassee
1224 Eppes Drive
Tallahassee, 32304
(850) 575-4477

*Caring People Ministries
5207 Mason Dixon Ave.
Bowling Green, 33834
(863) 375-3377
Mark Parker

Central Care Mission
4027 Lenox Blvd.
Orlando, 32811
(407) 299-6146
Herb

*AGAPE Family Ministries
22790 SW 122 Ave.
Miami-Dade 33170
(305) 235-2616
Sherri King

Bridges of America
206 Pilaklakaha Ave.
Auburndale, 33823
(863) 967-3295
Netza Rodriguez

Bridges of America
302 SW 2nd Street,
Unit 1
Pompano Beach, 33060
(954) 881-1029
Ginery Twichell

**Family Crisis Help
Center, Inc.**
1221 Kennedy Road,
Daytona Beach, 32114
(386) 255-0108
Ruth Plummer

Faith Farm Ministries
9538 Highway 441,
Boynton Beach, 33437
(561) 733-7256

1st Step Sober House
72 East McNabb Road
Pompano Beach 33060
(954) 942-7414
Program Director, S.
Randall Merritt

Florida Prison Ministries
2205 SE 45th Terrace
Gainesville, 32641
(352) 339-4732
Jeff Cobb

**Fresh Start Ministries
of Central Florida, Inc.**
4436 Edgewater Drive
Orlando, 32804
(407) 293-3822
Patricia

Good News – Mercy House
3418 Meridian Road
Tallahassee, 32312
(850) 383-1572
Brother Roberte

Harbor House Group, Inc.
7801 N. Hilburn Road
Pensacola, 32503
(850) 473-9603
Ed Noone

***Honesty House
Transitional Housing**
Hollywood, 33023
(954) 962-0670
Scott Friedman

**House of Hope of Alachua County,
Inc., Men's House**
21 SE 21st Street
Gainesville, 32641
(352) 376-3964
Thomas Johnson

***House of Hope of Alachua County,
Inc., Women's House**
2005 E University Ave.
Gainesville, 32641
(352) 376-3962
Joanna Lee

Jacksonville Re-Entry Center
1024 Superior Street
Jacksonville, 32254
(904) 588-0164

**Jim Russo Prison
Ministries, Inc.**
2106 26th Ave. East
Bradenton, 34208
(941) 746-3717
Ron Luke

**Ken Cooper Prison
Ministry (KCPM), Inc.**
Post Office Box 77160
Jacksonville, 32226
Ken Cooper

**Lamb of God
Ministries, Inc.
Okeechobee**
1012 S Parrott Ave.
Okeechobee, 34974
(863) 467-2677
Mike Lewandowski
Pompano Beach
971 S Dixie Highway
Pompano Beach 33060
(863) 467-2677
Mike Lewandowski

*Accepts Females

*Living Hope International Ministries, Inc.
801 29th Street
Orlando, 32805
(407) 422-6797
Marilyn Owens

Next Level Outreach
50 NE 49th Street
(mailing address) P.O.
Box 2763) Ocala, FL
34478
(352) 281-362

*Noah Community Outreach
3305 E 24th Avenue
Tampa, 33605
(813) 248-4408
Florence Gainer

One Unique Transition, Inc.
402 East Palm Avenue
Tampa, FL 33602
(704) 277-8714 or
(813) 270-3941

Passport to Success
13542 N. Florida Ave.
Suite 111, Tampa 33613
(813) 987-6700

Pathway to Change
P.O. Box 510818
Punta Gorda, 33951
(941) 639-2914 or
(239) 823-2911

Phoenix House
15681 N. U.S. Hwy 301
P.O. Box 1317
Citra, FL 32113
(352) 595-5000
exts. 6740 (John Velez),
6712 (Craig), or 6743
Admissions
FAX#
(352) 595-8431

Positive Images
2700 W. Oakland Park
Blvd.
Oakland Park, 33311
(954) 484-1824
(female only)

Prisoners of Christ
2nd Chance Apts.,
1715 Blvd.
Jacksonville, 32206
(904) 358-8866
Dan Palmer

Prisoners of Christ, Jericho House
1059 East 9th Street
Jacksonville, 32206
(904) 353-5237
Dan Palmer

Prisoners of Christ, Victory House
318 West 22nd Street
Jacksonville, 32206
(904) 359-9077
Dan Palmer

*Resurrection Ranch Ministries
5925 Old Dixie Highway
Melbourne, 32940
(321) 259-4970
Vaike Burton

*Salvation Army Jacksonville
900 West Adams
Jacksonville, 32204
(904) 358-8641
Cinda Bevell

Salvation Army St. Petersburg,
310 14th Ave. South
St. Petersburg, 33701
(727) 821-9123
J. Miller

*Sanctuary Mission
7463 W. Grover Cleveland Blvd.
Homosassa, 34446
(352) 621-3277
Byron Goldstein

The Sanctuary
P.O. Box 8463
Delray Beach, 33483
(561) 278-2797
(561) 247-5461
Byron Goldstein

*Second Chance
P.O. Box 8756
Lakeland, 33806
(863) 665-7700
Teresa Kemp

Second Change Training Center
825 Plum Street
Lakeland, 33801
(863) 686-1300 or
(863) 698-6105
(female only)

*Sober Living in Delray
220 SE 10th St. #301A
Delray Beach, 33483
(561) 279-8900
Sue Taylor

*Salus Care
3763 Evans Ave. #202
Ft. Myers, 33901
(239) 332-6937
Michelle Phillips

Sunset House
8800 Sunset Dr., Palm
Beach Gardens, 33410
(561) 627-9701
Mike Gordon

Steps To Serenity
7163 SW 14th Court
Lauderdale, FL 33315
(754) 214-0850
Director, Shawn Bateza

T.H.O.R.M, Inc.
3450 Dunn Avenue Ste. 303
Jacksonville FL 32218-6427
(904) 354-2233
Executive Director,
Dr. Cassandra Bush

*Transitions Recovery
Program
1928 NE 154 Street, #100
North Miami Beach, 33162
(305) 949-9001
Lee Barchan

Trinity Rescue Mission
622 West Union Street
Jacksonville, 32202
(904) 355-1205

*Accepts Females

FOR MORE
INFORMATION ABOUT
THE FLORIDA COMMISSION
ON OFFENDER REVIEW, OR
TO INQUIRE ABOUT A
CASE THAT INVOLVES
YOU, PLEASE CONTACT

**The Florida Commission on
Offender Review**
4070 Esplanade Way
Tallahassee, FL 32399-2450
Attn: Commission Clerk
Toll Free: (855) 850-8196
or (850) 487-3259
Fax: (850) 921-8712

DEFINITIONS

Advocate: (*verb*) To speak or write in favor of; support or urge by argument; recommend publicly; (*noun*) A person who pleads for or in behalf of another; intercessor.

Affidavit: A written declaration made under oath made before an authorized official.

Aggravating Factor: Any fact or circumstance that increases the severity or culpability of a criminal act.

Appeal: Applying to a higher court for a reversal of the decision of a lower court. There are five courts of appeal in Florida, plus the Supreme Court of Florida.

Board of Executive Clemency (BOEC): The governor, attorney general, chief financial officer and commissioner of agriculture. All are elected statewide and limited to two consecutive four-year terms.

Capital Felony: A crime punishable by death or life imprisonment without parole.

Charging instrument: Usually a document called a "criminal information" filed by a prosecutor that explains the formal charges; can also be a grand jury indictment.

Clemency: An act of mercy that absolves an individual from all or any part of the punishment that the law imposes.

Commission Action: The formal legal document that describes the decisions made at the hearing by the Florida Commission on Offender Review.

Commutation of Sentence: A type of clemency, a Commutation of Sentence may adjust an applicant's penalty to one less severe but does not restore any civil rights, nor does it restore the authority to own, possess, or use firearms.

Condition Precedent: An event that must take place before something else can happen.

Conditional Medical Release: The release of an inmate from incarceration by the Florida Commission on Offender Review when the inmate has been referred by the Department of Corrections, because of an existing medical or physical condition, which will either lead the inmate to be permanently incapacitated or terminally ill.

Conditional Release: All offenders whose crimes were committed on or after October 1, 1988, which crime fell under the violent offense categories of the Florida Rules of Criminal Procedure, and have served at least one prior felony commitment at a state or federal correctional institution, or have been sentenced as a habitual, violent habitual, violent career criminal or a sexual predator must be supervised under this program. This is NOT a discretionary early release program. When the qualifying offender is released by virtue of awards of gain time, the commission imposes appropriate terms and conditions of supervision until the end of the court-imposed sentence.

Confidential Case Analysis: The staff report for a clemency application prepared by the parole examiner and adopted by a majority of commissioners as an advisory recommendation for the Board of Executive Clemency (BOEC).

Effective Interview: The purpose of this hearing is to determine if the inmate will be granted parole. The commission can elect to grant parole, extend the Presumptive Parole Release Date (PPRD), or decline to authorize parole (placing the PPRD in a suspended status).

Effective Parole Release Date (EPRD): The actual parole release date authorized by the commission.

Exceptional Merit: The standard under Rule 17 to get a clemency case expedited.

Executive Clemency: The clemency function is an act of mercy that absolves an individual from all or any part of the punishment that the law imposes. This is a power to grant full or conditional pardons, or commute punishment. There are rules for these lengthy procedures, and these powers are vested in the governor only with the agreement of two cabinet members who are also statewide elected officials.

Extraordinary Interview: When the Presumptive Parole Release date is in suspended status, the inmate receives an Extraordinary Interview. The purpose of this hearing is to determine if the inmate's Presumptive Parole Release Date (PPRD) should be removed from a suspended status. The commission can elect to make no change in the PPRD or establish an Effective Parole Release Date (EPRD) within the next two years.

Extraordinary Review: A further examination by the commission of the entire record in an inmate's case following the commission's decision declining to authorize an Effective Parole Release Date.

Faith-and-Character-Based Institutions (FCBIs): Entire correctional facilities devoted to the Faith-and-Character-Based Correctional Initiative. Eligible inmates volunteer for FCBIs without regard to religion and can choose among secular or religious programming.

FCOR: Florida Commission on Offender Review.

FDOC: Florida Department of Corrections.

Felon: A person who has been convicted of a felony, which is a crime punishable by death or a term in state or federal prison.

Felony: A crime sufficiently serious to be punishable by death or a term in state or federal prison, as distinguished from a misdemeanor which is only punishable by confinement to county or local jail and/or a fine.

First Degree Murder: The unlawful killing of a human being when premeditated, or when committed by a person engaged in an unlawful act as defined in Fla. Stat. § 782.04. First degree murder constitutes a capital felony.

Florida Commission on Offender Review: (Formerly the Florida Parole Commission.) A group of three commissioners who make post-release decisions affecting inmates and ex-offenders. The commission functions as a quasi-judicial body. It also investigates clemency applications and makes advisory recommendations.

Florida Department of Corrections: The department charged with oversight of Florida inmates in its state prisons (including seven private prisons), and supervision of almost 146,000 active offenders on community supervision at probation offices throughout the state.

Florida Parole Commission: Created in 1941; in 2014 the name was changed to the Florida Commission on Offender Review.

Full Pardon: This is a type of clemency. A full pardon unconditionally releases a person from punishment and forgives guilt for any Florida convictions. It restores to an applicant all the rights of citizenship possessed by the person before his or her conviction, including the right to own, possess, or use firearms.

Initial Interview: At this hearing, parole will not be considered. The purpose of this hearing is to establish a Presumptive Parole Release Date (PPRD) and the Next Interview Date (NID). The commission evaluates many factors in establishing the PPRD.

Inmate: Any person under Florida Court Commitment to incarceration in any state or federal correctional facility, the Department of Corrections or to a county jail for a cumulative sentence of 12 months or more.

Institutional Conduct Record: The inmate's prison behavior, including disciplinary reports.

Matrix Time Range: The appropriate range of months found where the offender's salient factor score total intersects with the offender's severity of offense behavior.

Mitigation: Reduction of the matrix time range or the previously established presumptive parole release date.

Non-Advanceable Date: An inmate's release date that is restricted from continuous, monthly gain time awards over the entire length of sentence

Objective Parole Guidelines: Established in 1981, there are six main criteria upon which parole decisions are made.

Offense Severity Level: The statutorily assigned degree of felony or misdemeanor for the present offense of conviction.

Office of Executive Clemency: The coordinator and staff who administers the clemency process, including the quarterly public meetings at the state Capitol.

Parole: The release of an inmate, prior to the expiration of the inmate's sentence, with a period of supervision to be successfully completed by compliance with the enumerated conditions and terms of the release agreement as ordered by the commission. The decision of the commission to parole an inmate shall represent an act of grace of the state and shall not be considered a right.

Parole Supervision Review: The purpose of this hearing is to review the parolee's progress while on parole. The commission may elect to make no change or modify the reporting schedule and/or conditions of parole and schedule the next review date.

Parolee: An inmate placed on parole.

Parole Examiner: A commission staff member who interviews the inmate in prison, prepares a summary report, and makes a recommendation.

Perjury: The offense of willfully telling an untruth in a court after having taken an oath or affirmation.

Plea: A formal statement by or on behalf of a defendant or prisoner, stating guilt or innocence in response to a charge, offering an allegation of fact, or claiming that a point of law should apply.

PPRD: A Presumptive Parole Release Date (PPRD) is a tentative parole release date as determined by objective parole guidelines.

Probable Cause Affidavit: A sworn statement by a law enforcement officer that triggers an arrest. It describes the alleged facts and what specific laws were violated.

Probation: The release of a defendant for a period of supervision to be successfully completed by compliance with the enumerated conditions and terms of the release agreement as ordered by the trial court.

Program Participation: Inmate achievements and courses for work, education, vocational, spiritual, literacy and substance abuse programs.

Recidivism: A return to prison, which may be a result of a new conviction or a violation of post-prison supervision.

Restoration of Civil Rights: Another type of clemency, the Restoration of Civil Rights (RCR) restores to an applicant all of the rights of citizenship in the State of Florida enjoyed before the felony conviction, except the specific authority to own, possess, or use firearms. Such restoration shall not relieve an applicant from the registration and notification requirements or any other obligations and restrictions imposed by law upon sexual predators or sexual offenders.

Revocation Hearing: This hearing occurs when an offender is alleged to have violated the conditions of his/her release. When the commission finds the releasee guilty of a willful and substantial violation, the commission may order the violator returned to state prison to complete service of the original term of imprisonment.

Salient Factor Score: The indices of the offender's present and prior criminal behavior and related factors found by experience to be predictive in regard to parole outcome.

Severity of Offense Behavior: The statutorily assigned degree of felony or misdemeanor for the present offense of conviction.

Specific Authority to Own, Possess or Use a Firearm: Another type of clemency, this restores to an applicant the right to own, possess, or use firearms that were lost as a result of a felony conviction. Due to federal firearms laws, the Clemency Board will not consider requests for firearm authority from individuals convicted in federal or out-of-state courts. In order to comply with the federal laws, a Presidential Pardon or a Relief of Disability from the Bureau of Alcohol, Tobacco, Firearms and Explosives must be issued in cases involving federal court convictions. A pardon or restoration of civil rights with no restrictions on firearms must be issued by the state where the conviction occurred.

Spousal Immunity: Under the Federal Rules of Evidence, in a criminal case the prosecution cannot compel the defendant's spouse to testify against him. This privilege only applies if the defendant and the spouse witness are currently married at the time of the prosecution. Additionally, this privilege may be waived by the witness spouse if he or she would like to testify.

Subsequent Interview: The purpose of this hearing is to determine if any change should be made in the Presumptive Parole Release Date (PPRD) and establish the Next Interview Date (NID). The commission can elect to make no change, reduce or extend the PPRD.

Supreme Court of Florida: The highest appellate court in Florida, comprised of seven members appointed by the governor.

Transitional Housing: Facilities in the community designed to ease the transition of an offender from a correctional institution to living independently in the community while providing treatment, education, counseling, job training and placement, and transitional living opportunities.

Trial: The examination of facts and law presided over by a judge (or other magistrate, such as a commissioner or judge pro tem) with authority to hear the matter (jurisdiction).

Waiver: The intentional and voluntary giving up of something, such as a right, either by an express statement or by conduct (such as not enforcing a right).

Work Release: The Florida Department of Correction's (FDOC) Community Work Release program.

ACKNOWLEDGMENTS

Many thanks to:

Tallahassee attorney and lobbyist, Pamela Burch Fort, who in 2007 encouraged me to start writing and speaking about criminal justice issues.

Best-selling author, Vic Johnson, who is an internet marketing and publishing expert.

Author and nutrition expert, Lisa Johnson, for her cover ideas.

Graphic designer, Joni McPherson, of Iowa for creating the front and back covers.

Lynn McCartney and Mary Jo Stresky for proofreading and editing.

Deceased Tampa attorney, Marcelino J. "Bubba" Huerta, III, who referred to me my first clemency case in 1994.

Elected Public Defender, Nancy Daniels, of Tallahassee for recruiting me to present our first parole case in 2011.

Governors Lawton Chiles (deceased), Jeb Bush, Charlie Crist and Rick Scott and their clemency lawyers Mark Schlakman, Reg Brown, Circuit Judge Wendy Berger, Circuit Judge Vicki Brennan, County Judge Rob Wheeler, Drew Atkinson, and Bo Winokur.

Current and former cabinet members and their clemency lawyers and aides.

Current and former parole commissioners and their staffs.

On the Felix Garcia case, special thanks to his pro bono team:

Paralegal, Pat Bliss, of Virginia, and Colorado attorney, Jamie Jackson, for co-authoring Chapter Ten.

Super lobbyist, Brian Ballard, and his savvy partner, Greg Turbeville, of Ballard Partners in Florida for their strategic advocacy.

Ron Sachs, Michelle Ubben, and Porsche Haynes of Sachs Media Group in Tallahassee for generating excellent news coverage and social media awareness.

The author used publicly available information from various Florida government departments and agencies.

Information included in Chapters 2, 4 and 5 previously appeared in legal articles published in *Florida Defender*, a magazine publication of the Florida Association of Criminal Defense Lawyers.

ENDNOTES

Chapter Two:

1 Unless otherwise noted, all rule citations are to the Florida Rules of Executive Clemency (Fla.R.EX.C.), effective March 9, 2011.

2 Governor Scott's Remarks Prepared for Delivery, March 9, 2011.

3 Florida Commission on Offender Review website, section on Executive Clemency Historical Information.

Chapter Four:

4 FLA. STAT. § 947.002(5) (1997).

5 Id.

6 Florida Parole Commission, History of the Florida Parole Commission: Seven Decades of Service to the State. https://fpc.state.fl.us/History.htm (last visited Sept. 19, 2013); In re Rules of Criminal Procedure (Sentencing Guidelines), 439 So.2d 848, 849 (Fla. 1983).

7 Stop Turning Out Prisoners Act, ch. 294, § 4(1), 1995 Fla. Laws 2717, 2718; FLA. STAT. § 775.082(1) (2011).

8 FLA. STAT. § 947.02 (1997); FLA.STAT. § 947.03 (2000); FLA. STAT. § 947.04 (2001).

9 FLA. STAT. § 947.03(1) (2000).

10 FLA. STAT. § 947.04(1) (2001).

11 FLA. STAT. § 947.06 (2010).

12 FLA. ADMIN. CODE ANN. R. 23-21.006 (2010).

13 FLA. ADMIN. CODE ANN. R. 23-21.012 (2006).

14 FLA. ADMIN. CODE ANN. R. 23-21.013 (2013); FLA. STAT. § 947.174 (2013).

15 FLA. ADMIN. CODE ANN. R. 23-21.015 (2006).

16 FLA. ADMIN. CODE ANN. r. 23-21.0155 (2013).

17 FLA. ADMIN. CODE ANN. r. 23-21.0161 (2006).

18 FLA. STAT. § 947.19 (1997).

19 Email from Jennifer Dale, Administrative Assistant, Office of the General Counsel, Fla. Commission on Offender Review, to author's assistant (September 30, 2014 4:48PM EST) (on file with author).

20 Act of June 26, 1978, ch. 417, § 13(2), 1978 Fla. Laws 1381, 1381; FLA. STAT. § 947.005 (8) (2010); FLA. STAT. § 947.165 (1) (2013); FLA. STAT. § 947.172 (1997).

21 Act of June 26, 1978, ch. 417, § 12(1), 1978 Fla. Laws 1381, 1381; FLA. STAT. § 947.001 (1978); FLA. STAT. § 947.165 (2013).

22 Id.

23 FPC Policy Memorandum entitled "Objective Parole Guidelines" by and for the Fla. Parole Comm'n (undated) (on file with the Fla. Parole Comm'n).

24 FLA. STAT. § 947.172 (1997); FLA. STAT. § 947.173 (1973).

25 FLA. STAT. § 947.18 (2008).

26 Id.

27 Ch. 2013-119, Laws of Fla.

28 Art. IV § 8 (a) FLA. CONST. (1968).

29 WILLIAM H. BURGESS III, EXECUTIVE CLEMENCY - RULES OF EXECUTIVE CLEMENCY § 12:28 (1) (2011), available at https://1. next.westlaw.com/Document/I254d453ad07b11df9795ece435ab07fa/ View/FullText.html

30 Florida Parole Commn, *Commutation of Sentence Cases Granted 1980 Through April 30, 2013,*https://fpc.state.fl.us/PDFs/ CommutationofSentences1980-2013.pdf (last visited Sept. 19, 2013).

Chapter Five:

31 FDOC Annual Report, FY 2012-2013, December 2013, http://www. dc.state.fl.us/pub/annual/213/AnnualReport-1213.pdf

32 Email from FDOC, Office of General Counsel, dated 7/24/2014.

33 Florida Administrative Code (F.A.C.) Rule 33-601.602(1)(c).

34 F.A.C. 33-601.602(1)(b).

35 FDOC Website: www.dc.state.fl.us/. "Frequently Asked Questions."

36 F.A.C. Rule 33-601.210

37 F.A.C. Rule 33-601.602(2)(b).

38 F.A.C. Rule 33-601.602(1)(h)

39 F.A.C. Rule 33-601.602 (2)(c)

40 F.A.C. Rule 33-601.602 (2)(a)

41 Fla. Stat. §945.092.

42 FDOC Annual Report, FY 2012-2013, December 2013, pages 6-8.

43 PRIDE Enterprises 2013 Annual Report

44 FDOC Annual Report, FY 2012-2013, December 2013, pages 25-26.

45 ibid., page 27.

46 Ch. 2014-193, L.O.F., effective 7/1/2014 (CS/CS/HB 53).

47 Ch. 2013-040, L.O.F., effective 7/1/2013 (SB 1500, The General Appropriations Act, Item 662 "budget proviso."

Chapter Six:

48 Email from Florida Commission on Offender Review, Office of the General Counsel, dated 9/18/2014.

49 F.A.C. Rules 23-24.020 through 23-24.060.

Chapter Ten:

50 See Evidentiary Hearing Transcript at 74, Case No. 2D07-5750 (Fla. 2d D.C.A. Oct. 29, 2008) [hereinafter Evidentiary Hearing Transcript].

51 Evidentiary Hearing Transcript at 100-101.

52 Trial Transcript at 326–7, Garcia v. State, 453 So.2d 50 (Fla. 2d D.CA. 1984) [hereinafter Felix Trial Transcript].

53 Per a Gallaudet University test for the deaf and hard-of-hearing administered to Felix in 1999.

54 Affidavit of Frank Garcia (May 4, 1989).

55 Affidavit of Frank Garcia (1996).

56 Affidavit of Tina Daniels (September 10, 1996).

57 Evidentiary Hearing Transcript at 75, 86.

58 Id. at 84.

59 Letter from Frank Garcia to Felix Garcia (Jun. 3, 2010).

60 Evidentiary Hearing Transcript at 54.

Coming Soon!

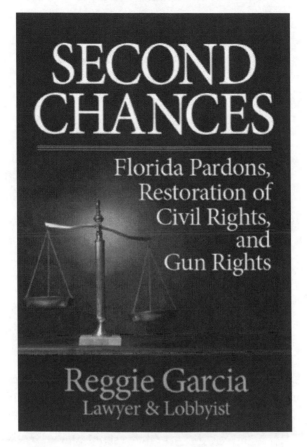

SECOND CHANCES
FLORIDA PARDONS, RESTORATION OF CIVIL RIGHTS, AND GUN RIGHTS

Excerpt and Advance of Chapter Three

Full Pardons

A "commutation of sentence" is the hardest type of clemency to obtain because it releases an inmate early from prison. The second hardest type of clemency is called a "full pardon" because it also restores firearm authority.

> Per Rule 4.I.A.: A full pardon unconditionally releases a person from punishment and forgives guilt for any Florida convictions. It restores to an applicant all of the rights of citizenship possessed by the person before his or her conviction, including the right to own, possess, or use firearms.

An applicant must wait ten (10) years from the conclusion of prison or probation, whichever is last, before seeking a full pardon. Probation can be instead of or after state prison.

In their first terms between 2011 and 2014, Florida Governor Rick Scott and the members of the Florida Cabinet approved 88 full pardons.

I successfully argued and helped obtain two full pardons during this period for two out- of-state business owners who committed felonies when they were younger.

Obtaining a full pardon has many benefits: It can help a felon to get state or federal licenses; security clearances; government contracts; better jobs; and even volunteer opportunities at school or with non-profit organizations.

It is the ultimate "second chance" where the state's top four elected officials recognize that someone has turned their life around and is now a productive citizen.

For example ... (successful case studies to be added when book is completed)

Made in the USA
Lexington, KY
30 May 2015